Winning the
MARKET GAME

Adedeji Sunmola

Copyright © 2024 ADEDEJI SUNMOLA

All rights reserved. No part of this book may be reproduced in any form without permission from the author or publisher.

A catalogue record for this book is available at the National Library of Nigeria

Table Of Contents

Preface .... **IV**
Foreword .... **VIII**
Introduction .... **X**

Chapter 1: The Psychology Of Winning 1
Chapter 2: Laying The Groundwork 15
Chapter 3: Crafting A Winning Strategy 22
Chapter 4: Tools Of The Trade 32
Chapter 5: Risk Management Mastery 43
Chapter 6: Timing The Market 54
Chapter 7: Building A Resilient Portfolio 66
Chapter 8: Advance Trading Techniques 78
Chapter 9: Learning From The Greats 88
Chapter 10: The Long Game 104

Reviews **115**
About The Book **117**
About The Author **118**

Preface

The stock market has always been more than numbers flashing on a screen or an abstract economic concept. For centuries, it has represented opportunity, a way to build wealth, achieve financial independence, and even shape legacies. Yet, for many, the market feels like an impenetrable fortress, a place where only the wealthy or the lucky seem to thrive. The truth is, this perception, while common, is fundamentally flawed. The market is not an exclusive club. It's a platform open to anyone with the willingness to learn, the discipline to act, and the patience to endure.

I remember my first encounter with the markets vividly. It was a chaotic blend of excitement and confusion. I watched as charts fluctuated wildly, headlines poured in at a relentless pace, and traders on the floor shouted frantically, their gestures and expressions filled with urgency. It was a sensory overload, yet I couldn't look away. I was mesmerized but also deeply intimidated. The questions came quickly: Could I ever understand this chaos? Could I ever win this game? Would I even belong in such a fast-paced, high-stakes world?

The answers didn't come immediately. In fact, they didn't come easily at all. The stock market is a world of noise and complexity, but beneath its surface lies a set of principles and patterns that, once understood, reveal its true nature. Over the years, I've learned that the key to unlocking its potential isn't about outsmarting the market or beating someone else, it's about mastering yourself. Success in the market demands clarity, discipline, and a mindset resilient enough to withstand the inevitable setbacks.

The truth is anyone can win the market game. Yes, anyone. It doesn't require insider knowledge, a Ph.D. in finance, or endless resources. What it does require is a willingness to learn, the humility to acknowledge what you don't know, and the courage to take calculated risks. The market rewards those who combine knowledge with discipline and approach it with both curiosity and caution.

This book isn't a promise of overnight SUCCESS. If you're looking for shortcuts or guarantees, you won't find them here. What you will find is a guide to understanding the market's rules, developing a strategy that aligns with your goals and strengths, and navigating the inevitable highs and lows with confidence. Along the way, I'll share the lessons I've learned through experience the wins that fueled my passion, the mistakes that humbled me, and the insights that helped me grow. You'll also hear the stories of others who've triumphed in their own market journeys, proving that success is attainable for anyone with the determination to pursue it.

Why does this matter? Because winning the market game can transform your life. It's not just about accumulating wealth; it's about creating opportunities. It's about achieving financial security, gaining the freedom to pursue your dreams, and building a foundation that supports both you and your loved ones. It's about breaking free from limitations whether they are financial, mental, or societal and stepping into a future you've consciously designed.

The market has a way of testing every participant, exposing weaknesses, and rewarding perseverance. But it's also a powerful teacher. Every rise and fall, every win and loss, carries lessons that go beyond dollars and cents. In mastering the market, you master decision-making, discipline, and emotional resilience skills that serve you in every area of life.

Whether you're a seasoned trader or just starting out, this book will equip you with the tools, knowledge, and mindset to thrive. It will challenge you to think differently, to embrace the unknown, and to see the market not as an adversary but as an opportunity. Together, we'll demystify its complexities and unlock its potential. The journey won't always be easy, but it will be worth it.

So, let's get started. This isn't just about winning financially it's about winning at life. It's about stepping into the role of architect for your future and embracing the possibilities that lie ahead. The market is a game, but it's one worth playing, and I'm here to show you how to play it well. Let's begin.

Foreword

The financial markets are a fascinating and ever-evolving landscape, offering opportunities for growth, wealth creation, and personal challenge. Yet, for many, they remain intimidating, a domain perceived as the playground of the privileged or the realm of inscrutable complexity. That's why *Winning the Market Game* is such an important and timely book. It demystifies the markets, making them accessible to anyone willing to learn and engage.

This book is not about shortcuts or guaranteed success. The author makes it clear: there are no magic formulas in the market. What you'll find here is something far more valuable, a roadmap for understanding the rules of the game, mastering your mindset, and navigating the markets with clarity and confidence. Drawing on years of experience and study, the author provides insights that will resonate with both beginners and seasoned investors alike.

What sets *Winning the Market Game* apart is its emphasis on the human element of investing and trading. While technical knowledge and strategy are essential, it is often our emotions; fear, greed, doubt, and overconfidence, that determine our success or failure. This book explores how to harness discipline, patience, and adaptability to make smarter decisions, even in the face of uncertainty. It's as much a guide to mastering yourself as it is to mastering the markets.

The lessons on these pages are timeless. Whether you're managing your retirement savings, building a diversified portfolio, or exploring active trading, this book offers tools and principles that will serve you for a lifetime. It doesn't promise overnight wealth, but it does promise a deeper understanding of the market and a path to achieving your financial goals.

If you're ready to take charge of your financial future and approach the markets with purpose and perspective, you've picked up the right book. The journey won't always be easy, but with *Winning the Market Game* as your guide, you'll be equipped to navigate the highs and lows and emerge stronger, wiser, and more successful.

Here's to your success in the market and beyond.

Introduction

The financial markets are among the most fascinating areas in the world. Every day, billions of dollars change hands as stocks rise, fall, and react to a myriad of forces, from earnings reports to geopolitical events. It's a vast, intricate system governed by the interplay of economics, psychology, and the collective behavior of millions of participants. To the uninitiated, this complexity can seem overwhelming, even impenetrable. But for those who take the time to understand it, the markets offer an extraordinary opportunity to grow wealth, test strategies, and engage with the dynamic forces that shape our global economy.

What exactly is "the market game"? At its core, it's a system of exchanges where individuals and institutions trade assets in hopes of achieving financial gains. Whether it's stocks, bonds, commodities, or currencies, every transaction is driven by a single, universal principle: buyers and sellers trying to agree on a price. Behind these transactions lie countless motivations investors seeking returns, companies raising capital, and traders speculating on future movements. Each trade, each decision, contributes to the market's ceaseless ebb and flow.

But to reduce the market game to mere numbers and transactions is to miss its essence. The market is fundamentally about people their emotions, decisions, and interactions. It's about psychology: the fear that drives panic selling, the greed that fuels speculative bubbles, the hope that keeps investors holding through volatility, and the despair that comes with a losing streak. It's about strategy: knowing when to act and when to wait, when to take risks and when to protect your capital. It's about adaptability: the ability to adjust to new information, unexpected events, and shifting market conditions. In short, the market game is as much about understanding human behavior as it is about financial analysis.

Like any game, the market has winners and losers. But unlike a traditional game, the market is not zero-sum. One trader's success doesn't necessarily come at the expense of another's. The market rewards those who are prepared, disciplined, and informed. It penalizes those who act impulsively, fail to manage risks, or neglect the importance of learning. Success in this area requires more than luck, it requires knowledge, patience, and the ability to make decisions under uncertainty.

This book is your playbook. It's designed to teach you the rules, strategies, and tools you need to play the market game effectively. You'll learn how to approach the market with a winning mindset, build strategies tailored to your goals, and manage the risks inherent in trading and investing. Whether you're interested in active trading, long-term investing, or simply understanding how the markets work, this book provides the foundation you need to succeed.

But let's address a common misconception upfront: this isn't about gambling or getting rich quick. The allure of overnight wealth has drawn many to the markets, only to see them leave disappointed and disillusioned. Winning the market game requires a long-term perspective, the discipline to stick to a plan, and the willingness to learn from both successes and failures. It's about making informed decisions based on analysis and logic, not emotion or speculation. It's about staying calm in the face of uncertainty, understanding that volatility is not a threat but an inherent feature of the market.

The journey to market success begins with understanding your "why." Why are you here? Are you looking to build a retirement fund, achieve financial freedom, or simply challenge yourself in a complex and rewarding environment? Your goals will shape your strategy and define your approach to the market. By clarifying what you want to achieve, you lay the groundwork for a focused and effective effort.

This book also emphasizes the importance of managing risks. Risk is an unavoidable part of the market game, but it doesn't have to be a barrier to success. By understanding how to assess and manage risks, you can make decisions with confidence, knowing that you are prepared for the challenges ahead. You'll learn how to protect your capital, evaluate opportunities, and strike a balance between caution and ambition.

Another key theme of this book is adaptability. The market is constantly changing, driven by technological advancements, economic shifts, and the ever-evolving behavior of its participants. What works today may not work tomorrow, and success often depends on your ability to adapt. By developing a mindset of continuous learning and improvement, you can stay ahead of the curve and turn challenges into opportunities.

Finally, this book is about empowerment. The markets are not just for professionals or those with vast resources. They are accessible to anyone willing to put in the effort to learn and grow. Whether you're a seasoned trader or a complete beginner, the principles and strategies outlined here will equip you with the tools to succeed.

Winning the market game is not just about financial gains, it's about building confidence, developing discipline, and creating opportunities for a better future. It's about taking control of your financial destiny and embracing the challenges and rewards that come with it. The journey won't always be easy, but with the right mindset and approach, it can be incredibly rewarding.

So, let's begin. Together, we'll demystify the market, explore its nuances, and unlock its potential. Whether you're here to secure your financial future, achieve a personal milestone, or simply better understand the world of finance, this book is your guide. The market is a game worth playing, and with the right preparation, it's a game you can win.

Chapter 1

THE PSYCHOLOGY OF WINNING

The financial markets are often described as a battlefield, but unlike traditional warfare, the most critical battles are fought within. For all the charts, algorithms, and sophisticated analysis tools available, the single most significant determinant of success or failure in the market is the trader's mind. The psychological game managing emotions, maintaining discipline, and overcoming biases is where the true challenge lies. It's no exaggeration to say that mastering the psychological aspect of trading is as important, if not more so, than mastering the technical or fundamental aspects.

Emotions are an inseparable part of human nature, and they influence every decision we make. In the context of the financial markets, emotions can swing wildly, often in reaction to market movements. A sudden spike in stock prices might evoke euphoria and lead to overconfidence, tempting traders to throw caution to the wind. Conversely, a sharp drop can ignite fear, causing panic-selling or hesitation when action is needed. These emotional reactions are not just the plight of beginners; even seasoned traders can fall victim to the powerful pull of human psychology. The key to winning is learning to recognize these emotional triggers and control them, rather than letting them control you.

Fear is perhaps the most pervasive emotion in trading. It manifests in several ways: fear of losing money, fear of missing out on an opportunity, and even fear of being wrong. This fear can lead to behaviors that undermine success, such as exiting a trade too early to lock in small profits or avoiding the market altogether after a series of losses. Fear thrives on uncertainty, and the financial markets are nothing if not uncertain. The antidote to fear is preparation. When traders have a well-thought-out plan and trust their strategy, they can act decisively even in uncertain conditions. Preparation provides a foundation of confidence that diminishes the grip of fear.

Greed, on the other hand, is the polar opposite of fear, yet equally destructive. It blinds traders to risk and fuels reckless behavior. The allure of quick and massive gains can lead to overleveraging positions, ignoring signs of trouble, or holding onto a position for too long in the hope of ever greater returns. The market is littered with the wreckage of traders who let greed guide their decisions. To counteract greed, successful traders cultivate a sense of discipline and contentment. They learn to stick to their plans, take profits at predetermined levels, and resist the temptation to chase after unattainable rewards.

Compounding the effects of fear and greed are the cognitive biases that subtly but profoundly shape decision-making. Cognitive biases are mental shortcuts our brains take, often leading to errors in judgment. One common bias is confirmation bias the tendency to seek out information that confirms our existing beliefs while ignoring evidence that contradicts them. In the market, this might mean clinging to a losing trade because you've convinced yourself that the stock will eventually rebound. Another prevalent bias is loss aversion, which causes people to feel the pain of losses more acutely than the pleasure of equivalent gains. This can lead to irrational behavior, such as holding onto losing trades for too long in the hope of avoiding a realized loss.

Overcoming these biases requires self-awareness and a commitment to objective analysis. Traders must be willing to confront their own tendencies and challenge their assumptions. One effective strategy is to keep a trading journal, recording not just the details of each trade but also the thought processes and emotions involved. Reviewing this journal regularly can reveal patterns of behavior and help traders identify areas for improvement.

Resilience is another essential trait for market success. Every trader experiences losses, it's an inevitable part of the game. What separates successful traders from the rest is their ability to recover and keep moving forward. Resilience is built by maintaining perspective, learning from mistakes, and staying consistent. It's about recognizing that no single trade, no matter how significant, defines your journey as a trader. It's about taking losses in stride, analyzing what went wrong, and using those lessons to refine your approach.

Building resilience also involves managing stress and maintaining a healthy balance. Trading can be mentally and emotionally taxing, especially during periods of high volatility or extended losses. To avoid burnout, traders must prioritize self-care. This includes setting realistic expectations, taking breaks when needed, and maintaining a life outside of the markets. A clear and rested mind is better equipped to make sound decisions.

The psychology of winning in the market is not about eliminating emotions but about mastering them. It's about cultivating a mindset that can withstand the highs and lows, remain disciplined in the face of temptation, and stay focused on long-term goals. Traders who achieve this level of mental mastery find themselves not only more successful in the market but also more confident and composed in all areas of life. Winning the market game begins with winning the battle within.

Winning the psychological battle also requires a shift in perspective about what "winning" truly means. Many people enter the market with the belief that success is about making as much money as possible, as quickly as possible. While profits are the ultimate goal, this mindset often leads to short-term thinking and high-risk behavior. True winners in the market understand that success is not about a single trade or even a streak of wins it's about consistency over time. They approach the market like a business, with a focus on process and discipline rather than chasing instant results.

One of the most powerful tools for developing this long-term perspective is setting clear and realistic goals. What do you want to achieve through trading or investing? Are you aiming to build a retirement fund, supplement your income, or grow wealth for future generations? Defining your objectives helps anchor your decision-making and prevents you from being swayed by the daily noise of the market. Once your goals are clear, you can create a plan to achieve them, a plan that aligns with your risk tolerance, time horizon, and personal circumstances.

Having a plan is crucial, but sticking to it is where the real challenge lies. The market is inherently unpredictable, and even the best-laid plans can be tested by unforeseen events. This is where discipline comes into play. Discipline means following your strategy even when emotions or external pressures tempt you to deviate. It means adhering to your risk management rules, taking profits when your targets are hit, and cutting losses when your stops are triggered. Traders who lack discipline often find themselves making impulsive decisions, chasing after losses, or deviating from their strategy in a desperate attempt to recover. In contrast, disciplined traders stay the course, trusting their plan and process even in turbulent times.

Another important aspect of winning the psychological game is learning to embrace uncertainty. Unlike many other endeavors, the financial markets offer no guarantees. Every trade carries a degree of risk, and even the most thorough analysis cannot eliminate the possibility of loss. For some, this uncertainty can be paralyzing. For others, it's a source of endless anxiety. The key is to reframe uncertainty not as something to be feared but as an inherent and even exciting part of the game. Accepting that you cannot control the market frees you to focus on what you can control: your decisions, your strategy, and your mindset.

Visualization and mindfulness are two techniques that can help traders navigate uncertainty and maintain focus. Visualization involves mentally rehearsing scenarios and responses before they occur. For example, imagine how you will react if a trade moves against you or if the market becomes highly volatile. By visualizing these situations and your ideal responses, you can train your mind to stay calm and execute your plan under pressure. Mindfulness, on the other hand, involves staying present in the moment and observing your thoughts and emotions without judgment. This practice can help you recognize when emotions are influencing your decisions and allow you to respond more thoughtfully.

A critical yet often overlooked element of psychological success is building a support system. Trading can be a lonely pursuit, particularly for independent traders who operate outside of traditional office environments. Having a network of fellow traders, mentors, or even just a trusted friend to talk to can make a significant difference. Sharing experiences, discussing challenges, and seeking advice can provide perspective and help you stay grounded during difficult times. A support system also offers accountability, as others can help you stay true to your goals and strategies.

Ultimately, winning the market game is about mastering yourself. It's about cultivating self-awareness, embracing discipline, and developing resilience. It's about finding a balance between confidence and humility, ambition and patience, risk-taking and caution. The journey to psychological mastery is not easy, and it's never truly complete. Even the most experienced traders must continually work to refine their mindset and stay vigilant against the pull of emotion and bias. But for those who are willing to put in the effort, the rewards both financial and personal are well worth it.

The mastery of self in the financial markets does not come overnight, nor does it come without challenges. Traders and investors must continuously evaluate their progress and refine their approach. This ongoing effort underscores the idea that winning the market game is a journey rather than a destination. It's a dynamic process that requires flexibility, adaptability, and a willingness to learn from both successes and failures.

One of the most critical aspects of this journey is the ability to detach emotionally from outcomes. This may sound counterintuitive; after all, profits and losses directly impact our financial well-being. However, emotional detachment is not about indifference; it's about maintaining objectivity. Traders who become overly attached to the outcomes of individual trades often find themselves trapped in cycles of euphoria and despair, which can cloud judgment and lead to impulsive decisions.

Instead of fixating on outcomes, focus on the process. Did you follow your strategy? Did you adhere to your risk management rules? Did you make decisions based on logic and data rather than emotion? By evaluating your performance in terms of process rather than profit, you shift your focus to what truly matters: consistent execution. Over time, consistent execution leads to consistent results.

This mindset is particularly important during periods of loss. Losses are an inevitable part of trading and investing, and no strategy can eliminate them entirely. What separates successful traders from unsuccessful ones is how they respond to losses. Many people view a loss as a failure, a personal shortcoming, or a reason to abandon their strategy. This perspective is not only unhelpful but also counterproductive. Losses are not failures; they are opportunities to learn. Every loss contains valuable information about the market, your strategy, and your own behavior. By analyzing your losses with a critical but constructive eye, you can uncover insights that will help you improve.

Conversely, periods of success can be just as dangerous as periods of loss. Winning streaks often lead to overconfidence, which can result in taking excessive risks or deviating from your plan. This phenomenon, known as the "winner's curse," has been the downfall of many traders. To avoid this trap, treat success with the same level of scrutiny as failure. Ask yourself whether your wins were the result of skill, luck, or a combination of both. Reflect on whether you adhered to your strategy or made decisions impulsively. This kind of self-reflection keeps you grounded and ensures that your success is sustainable.

Another critical element of psychological mastery is patience. The market is not a place for those seeking instant gratification. Building wealth through trading or investing takes time, and the most successful participants understand the value of waiting for the right opportunities. Patience is not passive; it is an active discipline. It means resisting the urge to act on every fluctuation in the market and instead waiting for setups that align with your strategy and criteria. Patience also means giving your investments the time they need to grow. Many great trades and investments fail not because they were poorly chosen, but because they were abandoned too soon.

This focus on patience ties into a broader principle: playing the long game. The financial markets are not a sprint; they are a marathon. Short-term gains are meaningless if they come at the expense of long-term sustainability. This is why successful traders and investors prioritize risk management above all else. Protecting your capital is the foundation of long-term success. No matter how enticing an opportunity may seem, if it involves risking more than you can afford to lose, it's not worth it. By prioritizing preservation over profits, you ensure that you'll be around to take advantage of future opportunities.

At the heart of playing the long game is the understanding that the market is a reflection of life itself. It is unpredictable, full of ups and downs, and often tests our patience, resilience, and discipline. But it also rewards those who are willing to put in the effort, take calculated risks, and adapt to changing circumstances. The lessons you learn in the market about managing emotions, making decisions under uncertainty, and persevering in the face of setbacks are lessons that can be applied to every aspect of your life.

Winning the market game is not just about accumulating wealth; it's about personal growth. It's about becoming more disciplined, more resilient, and more self-aware. It's about learning to think critically, act decisively, and take responsibility for your actions. And perhaps most importantly, it's about developing the confidence to trust yourself and the humility to keep learning.

The path to psychological mastery is not a straight line. It is a winding road with twists and turns, setbacks and breakthroughs. But with each step, you grow stronger, wiser, and more capable. And in the end, that growth is the true measure of success. Winning the market game begins with winning the battle within, and it is a battle that, with dedication and perseverance, you can win.

The process of mastering the psychological aspect of trading begins with acceptance. Accept that the market is unpredictable, accept that losses are inevitable, and accept that no strategy guarantees success in every situation. This acceptance is not an act of resignation but a foundation for growth. It allows you to move forward without the burden of unrealistic expectations, freeing your mind to focus on what truly matters: executing your plan, managing your risk, and maintaining your composure.

As you grow on your journey, you will notice subtle shifts in your mindset. Fear, once paralyzing, begins to feel manageable. Greed, once overwhelming, becomes easier to control. Setbacks, once devastating, transform into opportunities for reflection and improvement. These changes do not happen overnight, nor are they ever complete. Even the most seasoned traders experience moments of doubt or frustration. What separates them is their ability to acknowledge these moments without being consumed by them. They understand that every trade, every decision, every emotion is part of a larger process, a process that, when approached with discipline and patience, yields rewards over time.

Winning the psychological battle also requires an ongoing commitment to your well-being. Trading can be an intense and isolating pursuit, and the stress it generates can take a toll on your mental and physical health if left unchecked. To sustain long-term success, you must prioritize balance. This means stepping away from the screens when needed, engaging in activities that bring you joy, and maintaining a support network of friends, family, or fellow traders. A balanced trader is a focused trader, and a focused trader is one who wins.

The journey toward psychological mastery is deeply personal. It involves confronting your fears, acknowledging your biases, and committing yourself to continuous self-improvement. It is a journey that challenges not only your intellect but also your character. But as you cultivate the mindset of a winning trader, you will find that the rewards extend far beyond the financial. You will develop resilience, confidence, and a deeper understanding of yourself, qualities that will serve you well in every area of life.

With the foundation of psychological mastery in place, you are ready to explore the next essential element of market success: building a strong knowledge base. While psychology is the bedrock, understanding the mechanics of the market is the framework upon which you build your strategies and decisions. To truly win the market game, you must first understand the game itself.

Chapter 2

LAYING THE GROUNDWORK

The financial markets are vast, intricate, and ever evolving. They are a living system of interactions, where millions of participants; traders, investors, institutions, and governments converge to exchange assets, information, and capital. For those new to the game, this complexity can feel overwhelming. Stocks, bonds, commodities, derivatives each market has its own rules, rhythms, and participants. Yet, at their core, all markets operate on the same fundamental principle: supply and demand.

To navigate the market effectively, you must first understand its mechanics. This begins with familiarizing yourself with the different types of assets and their unique characteristics. Stocks represent ownership in a company and entitle shareholders to a portion of their profits. Bonds are debt instruments, where investors lend money to entities in exchange for periodic interest payments. Commodities include tangible goods such as gold, oil, and agricultural products, whose prices are influenced by global supply and demand. Derivatives, such as options and futures, are financial instruments whose value is derived from underlying assets, offering both opportunities for speculation and tools for risk management.

Each market operates within a broader ecosystem shaped by economic indicators, geopolitical events, and technological advancements. Understanding this ecosystem is critical to making informed decisions. For example, a rise in interest rates can affect bond prices, corporate profits, and consumer spending, creating ripple effects across multiple markets. Similarly, geopolitical tensions can disrupt supply chains, impact commodity prices, and alter investor sentiment. To thrive in this dynamic environment, you must stay informed, continuously updating your knowledge to reflect the ever-changing landscape.

Market cycles are another essential concept to grasp. These cycles comprising periods of expansion, peak, contraction, and trough are driven by the interplay of economic forces and investor behavior. Recognizing where we are in a cycle can provide valuable insights into potential opportunities and risks. For example, during a bull market, optimism often drives prices higher, presenting opportunities for growth-oriented investors. In contrast, a bear market may offer bargains for those with a long-term perspective and the courage to act when others are fearful.

Equally important is understanding the role of key players in the market. These include retail investors like you, institutional investors such as pension funds and mutual funds, and market makers who provide liquidity by buying and selling assets. Central banks, with their ability to influence interest rates and monetary policy, also play a significant role, as do governments through their fiscal policies and regulatory actions. Recognizing the motivations and behaviors of these players can give you a clearer picture of the forces driving market movements.

Knowledge is power, but only when applied effectively. As you delve deeper into the mechanics of the market, remember that your ultimate goal is not to become an encyclopedia of financial terms but to develop a practical understanding that informs your decisions. The market is a complex and dynamic system, but at its core, it is governed by patterns, principles, and human behavior. By mastering these fundamentals, you lay the groundwork for success preparing yourself to craft strategies, seize opportunities, and navigate challenges with confidence.

Building a strong foundation in market knowledge is more than an academic exercise; it is an essential step in becoming a confident and capable participant in the financial markets. Before diving into strategies or executing trades, you must first understand the mechanisms at play. The financial market is a vast, interconnected system, and every trade, investment, or decision you make will be influenced by its underlying structure.

At its heart, the market functions as a global auction. Buyers and sellers convene, either physically or digitally, to negotiate prices for assets. These assets span a wide range, including equities, fixed income, commodities, currencies, and derivatives. To navigate this auction effectively, you must understand what you are trading, who you are trading against, and the factors influencing their decisions. Each market has its own nuances, and failing to recognize these distinctions can be costly.

Take, for example, equities, or stocks. Stocks represent a share of ownership in a company, and their prices are influenced by a mix of company-specific factors, such as earnings and management decisions, and broader market trends, including interest rates and economic growth. Contrast this with bonds, which are essentially loans made to governments or corporations. Bond prices move inversely to interest rates, and their yields reflect the perceived risk of the borrower defaulting. Then there are commodities, whose prices are shaped by supply and demand dynamics, geopolitical events, and even weather patterns.

Derivatives add another layer of complexity. These financial instruments derive their value from an underlying asset, such as a stock, bond, or commodity. Options and futures, two common types of derivatives, can be used for speculation, hedging, or both. While they offer opportunities for profit, they also carry significant risks and require a deep understanding of their mechanics. Beginners often underestimate these risks, mistaking leverage for a shortcut to wealth. But leverage, while powerful, is a double-edged sword. It can amplify gains but also magnify losses, often to devastating effect.

Understanding these asset classes is only the beginning. The market operates within a broader ecosystem influenced by macroeconomic indicators, such as GDP growth, unemployment rates, and inflation. These indicators provide clues about the health of the economy and, by extension, the direction of markets. For instance, rising inflation often leads to higher interest rates, which can reduce corporate profitability and weigh on stock prices. Conversely, a strong jobs report may boost consumer confidence and spending, supporting economic growth and market performance.

The importance of market cycles cannot be overstated. Markets move in patterns of expansion and contraction, often mirroring the broader economic cycle. These cycles are driven by a combination of economic fundamentals and investor sentiment. During periods of economic growth, markets tend to rise as optimism prevails. However, when growth slows or contracts, fear often takes hold, leading to market declines. Recognizing these cycles and where we currently stand within them is crucial for timing your trades and investments. While no one can predict market movements with certainty, understanding the forces driving them can help you make more informed decisions.

The players in the market also wield significant influence. Retail investors, like individual traders and small-scale investors, are just one part of the ecosystem. Institutional investors, such as mutual funds, pension funds, and hedge funds, have far greater resources and often move markets with their trades. Market makers, who facilitate trading by providing liquidity, play a critical role in ensuring that markets function smoothly. Central banks, like the Federal Reserve, influence the market through monetary policy, while governments shape the landscape through fiscal policies and regulation. Understanding the motivations and behaviors of these players can provide valuable insights into market dynamics.

Equipped with this foundational knowledge, you are ready to move beyond the theoretical and into the practical. While understanding the market's mechanics is essential, it is only the first step. Winning the market game requires not only knowledge but also strategy, a plan tailored to your goals, risk tolerance, and unique strengths. In the next chapter, we will explore the process of crafting a winning strategy. This is where preparation meets execution and where your market journey begins in earnest.

Chapter 3

CRAFTING A WINNING STRATEGY

In the financial markets, knowledge is the foundation, but strategy is the blueprint. A well-crafted strategy is what separates deliberate decision-making from aimless speculation. It provides structure to your actions, guiding you through the chaos of market fluctuations and enabling you to navigate both opportunities and risks with clarity and confidence. Without a strategy, even the most well-informed trader is at the mercy of the market's unpredictability. With one, you take control turning uncertainty into calculated opportunity.

The first step in crafting a winning strategy is understanding that there is no one-size-fits-all approach. Successful strategies are as diverse as the people who create them. Some traders thrive on short-term volatility, seeking profits from rapid price movements, while others adopt a long-term perspective, focusing on steady growth and compounding returns. Some prefer the analytical rigor of fundamental analysis, digging into balance sheets and economic data, while others rely on the patterns and signals of technical analysis. The key is to define what works for you, based on your goals, resources, and temperament.

Start by identifying your objectives. Are you looking to generate short-term income, build long-term wealth, or perhaps a combination of both? Your objectives will shape the type of strategy you pursue. A day trader, for instance, focuses on capturing small, frequent gains by exploiting intraday price movements. This approach requires constant attention, quick decision-making, and a high tolerance for risk. On the other hand, a value investor seeks to buy undervalued assets and hold them for extended periods, allowing time for their intrinsic value to be realized. This approach demands patience, discipline, and a willingness to weather market fluctuations.

Once your objectives are clear, consider your risk tolerance. Every strategy involves trade-offs between risk and reward, and understanding your comfort level with risk is crucial for long-term success. Are you comfortable taking on higher risk for the potential of higher returns, or do you prefer a more conservative approach that prioritizes capital preservation? Your risk tolerance will influence everything from the types of assets you trade to the size of your positions and the frequency of your trades.

With your objectives and risk tolerance in mind, it's time to explore different trading and investing styles. If you're drawn to analyzing company performance, financial statements, and industry trends, a fundamentally driven approach might suit you. This could involve identifying undervalued stocks using metrics like price-to-earnings (P/E) ratios, dividend yields, or growth potential. Fundamental analysis focuses on the intrinsic value of assets, looking beyond market noise to uncover opportunities based on long-term potential.

Alternatively, if you're intrigued by price charts, patterns, and indicators, technical analysis may align with your strengths. Technical traders study historical price movements and trading volumes to identify trends, support and resistance levels, and potential breakout points. This approach is often favored by short-term traders, as it provides actionable insights for timing entries and exits with precision.

Hybrid strategies, combining elements of both fundamental and technical analysis, are also popular. For example, you might use fundamental analysis to identify promising stocks and then apply technical analysis to determine the optimal timing for buying or selling them. The beauty of crafting your own strategy is that you can tailor it to your unique strengths and preferences, drawing inspiration from various approaches while creating something uniquely yours.

Developing a strategy is only half the battle; testing and refining it is equally important. Before committing real capital, backtest your strategy using historical data to see how it would have performed under past market conditions. Many trading platforms offer back testing tools, allowing you to simulate trades and analyze results. While past performance is not a guarantee of future success, back testing can reveal strengths, weaknesses, and potential areas for improvement in your strategy.

In addition to back testing, consider starting with a demo account or paper trading. These tools allow you to practice implementing your strategy in real-time market conditions without risking actual money. Use this phase to refine your process, identify any gaps in your plan, and build confidence in your decision-making. Only when you've thoroughly tested your strategy and feel comfortable with its execution should you begin trading with real capital.

Even with a solid strategy, flexibility is essential. Markets are dynamic, and conditions can change rapidly. A strategy that works well in a bull market may falter during a downturn, and a method optimized for high volatility might struggle in calm conditions. Successful traders and investors are not rigid; they adapt their strategies to fit the prevailing environment while staying true to their core principles. This requires staying informed, continuously learning, and being willing to adjust your approach when necessary.

At its core, a winning strategy is about more than just making money, it's about creating a framework that aligns with your goals, values, and lifestyle. It's a tool that empowers you to navigate the markets with purpose and confidence, enabling you to seize opportunities while managing risks effectively. By defining your objectives, understanding your risk tolerance, and developing a strategy that plays to your strengths, you set the stage for consistent and sustainable success.

Creating a winning strategy begins with self-awareness. Before diving into specific methods or tools, take a step back to evaluate your strengths, weaknesses, and preferences. The financial markets are a vast ecosystem, and no one approach works for everyone. The more you understand about yourself; your tolerance for risk, your time commitment, and your decision-making style, the better equipped you'll be to build a strategy that suits you.

For example, if you're someone who thrives in fast-paced environments and make quick decisions, a short-term trading strategy like day trading or scalping might appeal to you. These approaches rely on rapid execution and the ability to capitalize on small price movements. However, they also demand a significant time commitment, constant focus, and a strong ability to manage stress. On the other hand, if you prefer a more analytical and deliberate pace, long-term investing strategies such as value investing or dividend growth investing might align better with your personality. These strategies require patience and a willingness to endure short-term volatility in pursuit of long-term gains.

Your financial situation and time availability are also critical considerations. Someone with a full-time job outside of trading may not have the bandwidth to monitor markets throughout the day. In such cases, swing trading a medium-term strategy that involves holding positions for several days or weeks, can offer a balance between active management and flexibility. Alternatively, if you have a long investment horizon and prefer a hands-off approach, building a diversified portfolio of index funds or ETFs might be the most practical path.

Once you have a clear sense of your personal preferences and constraints, the next step is to define your edge. Your edge is what sets you apart from other market participants. It could be a specific skill, such as the ability to analyze financial statements or identify chart patterns, or it could be a unique perspective, such as a deep understanding of a particular industry or market niche. Defining your edge is critical because it informs the choices you make and the strategies you pursue. Without an edge, you're essentially gambling, relying on luck rather than skill to generate returns.

A well-crafted strategy is built on three pillars: objectives, methodology, and risk management. Your objectives define what you're trying to achieve whether it's income generation, capital appreciation, or wealth preservation. Your methodology outlines how you plan to achieve those objectives, including the tools and techniques you'll use to analyze markets and execute trades. Finally, risk management is the safeguard that protects your capital and ensures you can weather the inevitable ups and downs of the market.

Risk management, in particular, deserves special attention. Many traders and investors focus primarily on returns, often at the expense of managing risk. However, protecting your capital is the foundation of long-term success. A single large loss can erase months or even years of gains, making it critical to have clear rules in place for managing risk. These rules should include position sizing determining how much capital to allocate to each trade, setting stop-loss levels to limit potential losses and diversifying your portfolio to reduce exposure to any single asset or market.

With your strategy framework in place, testing becomes the next crucial step. Back testing allows you to simulate your strategy using historical data, providing insights into its potential performance under various market conditions. While back testing cannot predict future outcomes, it can help you identify strengths and weaknesses, fine-tune your approach, and build confidence in your methodology. Most modern trading platforms offer back testing tools, and there are countless resources online to guide you through the process.

Paper trading, or trading in a simulated environment, is another valuable tool for testing your strategy. It allows you to practice implementing your plan in real-time market conditions without risking actual capital. Use this phase to identify any operational challenges, such as issues with timing or execution, and refine your process accordingly. Paper trading also helps you build the mental discipline needed to stick to your strategy, as it simulates the emotional experience of trading without the financial consequences.

Even after you transition to live trading, your strategy should remain a work in progress. Markets are dynamic, and what works today may not work tomorrow. Regularly review and evaluate your performance, keeping detailed records of your trades, including your reasoning, execution, and outcomes. This trading journal becomes an invaluable resource, offering insights into your strengths, areas for improvement, and patterns in your decision-making.

Adaptability is another hallmark of a successful strategy. While it's essential to have a clear plan, rigid adherence to a single approach can be detrimental in a changing environment. For instance, a trend-following strategy may excel in a bull market but falter during periods of consolidation or high volatility. Similarly, a value-oriented approach may underperform when growth stocks dominate the market. The ability to recognize when adjustments are needed and make those changes without losing sight of your overarching goals is a critical skill for any trader or investor.

Finally, crafting a winning strategy is about more than just mechanics; it's about mindset. A successful strategy is not just a set of rules; it's a framework for disciplined decision-making. It helps you stay focused on your objectives, maintain consistency in your actions, and avoid the emotional pitfalls that can derail even the best-laid plans. When you approach the market with a well-thought-out strategy, you position yourself not only to seize opportunities but also to weather challenges with confidence and resilience.

With a clear strategy in place, you are now ready to engage with the market on your terms. The next step is equipping yourself with the tools and resources needed to bring your strategy to life. In the following chapter, we will explore the essential tools of the trade from trading platforms and analytical software to news sources and market data and how to use them effectively to gain an edge in the market.

Chapter 4

TOOLS OF THE TRADE

No matter how well-crafted your strategy is, its success depends on your ability to execute it effectively. This is where tools come into play. In today's financial markets, traders and investors have access to a vast array of resources that were once the exclusive domain of large institutions. From sophisticated trading platforms to advanced analytical tools, these resources can help you analyze markets, identify opportunities, and execute trades with precision. However, with so many tools available, it's crucial to understand which ones align with your strategy and how to use them effectively.

The foundation of your trading toolkit is the trading platform you choose. This platform serves as your gateway to the markets, enabling you to execute trades, monitor positions, and access real-time market data. The best trading platforms offer a combination of user-friendly interfaces, robust features, and reliable execution. Popular platforms like MetaTrader, ThinkorSwim, and Interactive Brokers cater to a range of trading styles, from beginners to seasoned professionals. When selecting a platform, consider factors such as ease of use, available markets, and compatibility with your preferred devices. Many platforms also offer demo accounts, allowing you to familiarize yourself with their features before committing real capital.

In addition to a trading platform, charting software is an essential tool for technical analysis. Platforms like TradingView, NinjaTrader, and Bloomberg Terminal provide advanced charting capabilities, allowing you to visualize price movements, analyze trends, and identify key support and resistance levels. These tools often include a wide range of technical indicators, such as moving averages, RSI, and MACD, which can help you interpret market dynamics and make informed decisions. For those who rely on technical analysis, the ability to customize charts and indicators to suit your strategy is invaluable.

While charting tools are ideal for visualizing price action, fundamental analysis requires a different set of resources. Financial news platforms like Bloomberg, Reuters, and CNBC provide real-time updates on economic events, earnings reports, and market trends. Websites like Yahoo Finance, Morningstar, and Seeking Alpha offer in-depth company profiles, financial statements, and analyst insights. These resources are particularly valuable for long-term investors, as they provide the information needed to assess a company's intrinsic value and growth potential. For those focusing on macroeconomic trends, central bank announcements, economic calendars, and reports from organizations like the IMF and World Bank are indispensable.

Another powerful tool in your arsenal is a reliable data feed. Real-time market data is critical for making timely decisions, especially for short-term traders who need to react quickly to price movements. Many trading platforms include basic data feeds, but advanced traders may require additional data services for specific markets or assets. Subscribing to premium data feeds from providers like CQG, Trade Station, or Interactive Data Corporation can offer an edge by providing faster updates, more comprehensive information, or specialized analytics.

For traders and investors looking to automate their strategies, algorithmic trading tools are becoming increasingly accessible. Platforms like QuantConnect, MetaTrader's MQL5, and Interactive Brokers' API allow you to create and test custom trading algorithms. These tools can execute trades based on predefined criteria, removing the emotional element from decision-making and enabling you to take advantage of opportunities even when you're not actively monitoring the markets. However, algorithmic trading requires a solid understanding of programming and risk management, as poorly designed algorithms can lead to significant losses.

Risk management tools are another critical component of your toolkit. Position sizing calculators, for example, help you determine the optimal amount of capital to allocate to each trade based on your risk tolerance and account size. Stop-loss and take-profit orders, available on most trading platforms, allow you to automate your exit strategy, ensuring that your losses are limited, and your profits are secured. Portfolio tracking tools like Personal Capital, Mint, or Portfolio Visualizer provide a holistic view of your investments, helping you monitor diversification, performance, and risk exposure.

Beyond software and platforms, staying informed is key to success in the markets. Subscribing to financial newsletters, joining online forums, and participating in trading communities can provide valuable insights and keep you updated on the latest developments. However, it's essential to be discerning about your sources. Misinformation or biased opinions can lead to poor decision-making, so prioritize reputable and objective resources.

As you build your toolkit, remember that technology is a means to an end, not an end in itself. The tools you choose should complement your strategy, not dictate it. For example, if your strategy relies on long-term investing, there's little need for high-frequency trading software. Conversely, a day trader may prioritize tools that provide lightning-fast execution and real-time data. By aligning your tools with your goals and approach, you can maximize their value and avoid unnecessary complexity.

Finally, as technology continues to evolve, too will the tools available to traders and investors. Artificial intelligence, machine learning, and blockchain are just a few of the innovations shaping the future of finance. Staying informed about these trends and being open to adopting new technologies can provide a competitive edge in the ever-changing landscape of the market.

The tools at your disposal as a trader or investor are not merely conveniences; they are the bridge between theory and execution. Mastering these tools is essential to implementing your strategy effectively, minimizing errors, and responding to the ever-changing dynamics of the financial markets. However, with the vast number of tools available today, it's easy to feel overwhelmed. Understanding their functions, benefits, and limitations is key to building a streamlined, efficient, and personalized toolkit.

Your trading platform is the cornerstone of your operations. In addition to basic functionalities like placing trades and tracking orders, many platforms provide features that can enhance your decision-making. For instance, platforms like MetaTrader and ThinkorSwim offer advanced charting tools, real-time market data, and customization options that allow you to tailor the interface to your needs. The availability of mobile apps ensures you can monitor and manage your trades on the go, providing flexibility and accessibility.

Selecting the right platform depends on your specific trading style. If you're a day trader, you may prioritize speed of execution and advanced order types, such as conditional orders or algorithmic triggers. For long-term investors, access to detailed research reports, portfolio tracking, and tax planning features may take precedence. It's worth investing time to explore different platforms, using demo accounts to evaluate their features before committing to one.

Charting software is indispensable for traders who rely on technical analysis. Platforms like TradingView have revolutionized how traders interpret data, offering intuitive interfaces, a wide range of indicators, and the ability to share ideas with a global community. Advanced users might benefit from tools like NinjaTrader or Bloomberg Terminal, which provide deep customization options and integration with third-party analytics. The ability to annotate charts, back test strategies, and create alerts for specific price levels can save time and improve decision-making accuracy.

For fundamental analysis, access to comprehensive financial data is critical. Services like Morningstar and Value Line provide in-depth company reports, historical data, and industry comparisons. Earnings calendars, dividend trackers, and economic release schedules help investors stay on top of events that could influence their portfolios. Meanwhile, financial news platforms like Reuters, CNBC, and Bloomberg keep you updated on breaking news, corporate developments, and macroeconomic trends. Combining these resources with real-time data feeds ensures you have the information you need to make timely and informed decisions.

Real-time data feeds are particularly vital for active traders. These feeds provide up-to-the-second updates on prices, volume, and order flow, enabling you to react quickly to market movements. Providers like CQG and Interactive Data Corporation offer high-quality data streams that cater to professional traders, often with the added benefit of customizable analytics. For less time-sensitive strategies, delayed data may suffice, but for strategies that hinge on precision timing, investing in a robust data feed is a worthwhile expense.

Algorithmic trading tools have become increasingly popular among traders seeking to automate their strategies. By using platforms like QuantConnect or MetaTrader's MQL5, you can create algorithms that execute trades based on predefined criteria, such as technical signals, volume thresholds, or fundamental events. Algorithmic trading removes the emotional element from decision-making, ensuring that your strategy is executed consistently. However, it requires a strong understanding of both programming and risk management. Poorly designed algorithms can exacerbate losses, and even well-designed ones must be monitored to ensure they adapt to changing market conditions.

Risk management tools are just as important as tools for analysis and execution. Position sizing calculators, for instance, help you determine the appropriate amount of capital to allocate to a trade based on your risk tolerance and account size. This ensures that no single trade jeopardizes your portfolio. Stop-loss and take-profit orders, which can be set directly on most trading platforms, automate your exit strategy, protecting your capital and locking in profits even if you're not actively monitoring the market. For portfolio-level risk management, tools like Portfolio Visualizer allow you to assess diversification, stress-test your holdings, and simulate how your portfolio would perform under different market scenarios.

Education and community resources are another often-overlooked category of tools. Trading is a continuous learning process, and staying informed about market trends, new strategies, and emerging technologies is crucial. Joining online communities, subscribing to financial newsletters, and attending webinars or workshops can provide fresh perspectives and valuable insights. Platforms like Reddit's r/WallStreetBets, Seeking Alpha forums, and

Discord trading groups can connect you with like-minded traders, though it's important to approach these with discernment. The advice and strategies shared in these spaces can vary widely in quality, so always cross-reference information with reputable sources.

Finally, as technology evolves, new tools and resources are emerging that can provide additional advantages. Artificial intelligence and machine learning are increasingly being used to identify patterns, analyze sentiment, and predict market movements. Blockchain technology, meanwhile, is creating new opportunities in decentralized finance (DeFi) and tokenized assets. Staying ahead of these trends can give you a competitive edge, whether by leveraging AI-powered analysis tools or exploring investment opportunities in innovative sectors.

With all these tools at your disposal, the challenge lies in selecting and integrating them into a cohesive workflow. Start with the essentials: a reliable trading platform, charting software, and access to quality data. From there, add tools that complement your strategy and address specific needs, such as risk management or automation. Avoid the temptation to overcomplicate your setup with unnecessary gadgets or software. Simplicity and clarity are often more effective than an abundance of tools, especially when you're first starting out.

As you refine your toolkit, remember that tools are only as effective as the person using them. Invest time in learning how to use each tool to its full potential and continuously evaluate their performance in supporting your strategy. By combining the right tools with the right mindset, you create a powerful framework for executing your strategy and achieving success in the market.

With your toolkit ready, the next step is mastering the art of risk management. In the following chapter, we will delve into the principles and practices that safeguard your capital, enabling you to navigate the inevitable uncertainties of the market while staying focused on your long-term goals.

Chapter 5

RISK MANAGEMENT MASTERY

Risk management is the cornerstone of long-term success in the financial markets. While it's tempting to focus solely on strategies that maximize returns, the reality is that preserving capital is equally, if not more, important. The markets are unpredictable, and no strategy is immune to losses. Risk management ensures that when things go wrong, and they inevitably will you can recover and stay in the game.

At its core, risk management is about controlling the variables you can. You cannot control the market's movements, economic conditions, or unexpected news, but you can control how much you're willing to lose, how you allocate your capital, and when you decide to enter or exit a trade. This discipline is what separates successful traders and investors from those who let emotions and impulses dictate their decisions.

The first principle of risk management is understanding your risk tolerance. This is the level of risk you are comfortable taking based on your financial situation, goals, and psychological disposition. Risk tolerance varies from person to person and can be influenced by factors such as age, income, investment horizon, and personal preferences. Someone nearing retirement may prioritize capital preservation, while a young professional with a steady income may feel comfortable taking on higher risks for the potential of greater rewards.

Once you've determined your risk tolerance, the next step is position sizing, deciding how much capital to allocate to each trade or investment. A common rule of thumb is to risk no more than 1–2% of your total trading capital on any single trade. For example, if you have a $10,000 trading account and adhere to a 2% risk rule, you will risk no more than $200 on a single trade. This ensures that even a string of losses will not deplete your account, allowing you to stay in the market and recover.

Position sizing is closely tied to another critical tool: the stop-loss order. A stop-loss order is a predefined price level at which you exit a trade to limit your losses. Setting a stop-loss requires balancing risk and reward. Placing it too close to the entry point may result in being stopped out prematurely, while placing it too far away increases the potential for larger losses. The key is to align your stop-loss with your strategy, using technical or fundamental analysis to identify logical exit points.

For longer-term investors, diversification is a cornerstone of risk management. Diversification involves spreading your investments across different asset classes, industries, or geographic regions to reduce exposure to any single risk. For example, a portfolio that includes stocks, bonds, and real estate is less vulnerable to market-specific downturns than one concentrated solely in equities. Similarly, owning stocks in different sectors, such as technology, healthcare, and consumer goods, can mitigate the impact of sector-specific risks.

While diversification is a powerful tool, it's important not to over-diversify. Holding too many assets can dilute potential returns and make your portfolio difficult to manage. The goal is to strike a balance diversifying enough to reduce risk while maintaining focus on high-quality investments that align with your objectives.

Another critical aspect of risk management is understanding and controlling leverage. Leverage allows traders to amplify their exposure to the market by borrowing funds or using margin. While this can magnify gains, it also significantly increases the potential for losses. For example, a 10% loss on a leveraged position could result in a 50% reduction in your account balance, depending on the level of leverage used. Traders who use leverage must be especially disciplined, setting strict limits on position sizes and maintaining sufficient margin to avoid forced liquidations.

In addition to these tools, emotional discipline is a crucial element of risk management. Fear and greed can lead to impulsive decisions, such as exiting a trade too early to lock in small profits or holding onto a losing position in the hope of a rebound. To counteract these tendencies, establish clear rules for entering and exiting trades, and stick to them regardless of market conditions. Keeping a trading journal can help you track your decisions and identify patterns in your behavior, allowing you to refine your approach over time.

One of the most effective ways to manage risk is by thinking in terms of probabilities rather than certainties. No trade or investment is guaranteed to succeed, but every decision carries a probability of success based on your analysis. By focusing on the process rather than the outcome, you can make decisions with confidence, knowing that even if a trade doesn't work out, it was based on sound reasoning.

Another valuable mindset shift is viewing losses as part of the cost of doing business. Just as a retailer accepts the occasional loss from damaged goods, traders and investors must accept that losses are an inevitable part of the market. The goal is not to avoid losses entirely but to ensure that they are manageable and do not derail your long-term strategy. A well-managed loss is not a failure; it is a necessary step in the pursuit of success.

Advanced traders may also use hedging strategies to manage risk. Hedging involves taking offsetting positions to reduce exposure to adverse market movements. For example, an investor holding a portfolio of tech stocks might buy put options on a technology ETF to protect against a sector-wide downturn. While hedging can reduce risk, it often comes at a cost, such as reduced potential returns or additional fees. It's essential to weigh these trade-offs carefully and ensure that hedging aligns with your overall strategy.

Ultimately, risk management is about sustainability. The goal is not just to survive the inevitable setbacks but to thrive in the face of them. By protecting your capital, maintaining discipline, and continuously refining your approach, you build a foundation for long-term success. Risk is an inherent part of the market, but with the right tools and mindset, it becomes a challenge to navigate rather than a threat to fear.

Effective risk management isn't just a set of rules; it's a philosophy that underpins every decision you make in the market. It's about prioritizing longevity over short-term gains, understanding the inherent uncertainties of trading and investing, and taking proactive steps to mitigate potential losses. Whether you're a novice trader or an experienced investor, embracing a risk-first mindset can transform the way you engage with the markets and significantly improve your chances of long-term success.

At the heart of this philosophy is the principle of asymmetric risk-to-reward ratios. Every trade or investment you make should offer the potential for significantly greater rewards than the risks you are taking. For example, a risk-to-reward ratio of 1:3 means that for every dollar you risk, you stand to gain three. By consistently seeking trades with favorable risk-to-reward ratios, you can ensure that even if your success rate is less than 50%, you will still come out ahead over time. This approach shifts the focus from trying to win every trade to managing the overall profitability of your strategy.

One common mistake many traders and investors make is overconfidence during winning streaks. Success can create a false sense of security, leading to larger position sizes, excessive leverage, and lax adherence to risk management rules. This overconfidence can be especially dangerous during periods of heightened market volatility when unexpected reversals can quickly wipe out gains. The solution is to remain disciplined regardless of recent performance. Stick to your predetermined risk limits and avoid letting emotions dictate your decisions.

Conversely, losing streaks can test even the most seasoned traders. A series of losses can erode confidence, leading to hesitation, second-guessing, or impulsive attempts to recoup losses through aggressive trading. This emotional response, often referred to as "revenge trading," is one of the quickest ways to compound losses. To break this cycle, take a step back and reassess your approach. Review your strategy, analyze your trades to identify potential errors, and remind yourself that losses are a natural part of the market. Sometimes, the best course of action is to take a temporary break, allowing yourself time to regain perspective and clarity.

Another powerful concept in risk management is the idea of portfolio-level risk. While managing individual trades is important, it's equally critical to assess the overall risk exposure of your portfolio. Diversification is a key tool in this regard, but true diversification goes beyond simply owning a variety of assets. It involves ensuring that your portfolio is not overly reliant on a single market, sector, or geographic region. For example, holding stocks in both developed and emerging markets, or balancing equity exposure with fixed-income and alternative investments, can reduce your vulnerability to localized economic shocks.

Correlation is a crucial consideration when constructing a diversified portfolio. Assets that are highly correlated tend to move in the same direction under similar conditions, which can amplify risk during market downturns. By including assets with low or negative correlations such as gold, which often rises during equity market declines, you can create a portfolio that is more resilient to market fluctuations. Portfolio management tools and software can help you analyze correlations and optimize your asset allocation to achieve true diversification.

Stress testing your portfolio is another valuable risk management practice. This involves simulating how your portfolio would perform under various adverse scenarios, such as a sharp market correction, a spike in interest rates, or geopolitical turmoil. Stress testing provides insights into potential vulnerabilities and allows you to make adjustments proactively. Many portfolio management platforms include built-in stress-testing features, making it easier to evaluate your risk exposure and implement changes as needed.

Hedging is an advanced risk management technique that can provide additional protection during uncertain times. Common hedging instruments include options, futures, and inverse ETFs. For instance, buying put options on an index can serve as insurance against a broad market decline, while shorting individual stocks or sectors can offset potential losses in other parts of your portfolio. While hedging can reduce risk, it also comes with costs, such as premiums for options or margin requirements for short positions. It's important to weigh these costs against the potential benefits and use hedging selectively, based on your specific risk profile and market outlook.

Position scaling is another technique that can help you manage risk while optimizing returns. Scaling involves entering or exiting positions gradually rather than all at once. For example, instead of investing your entire allocation in a single stock at once, you might buy in smaller increments over time, allowing you to average your entry price and reduce the impact of short-term volatility. Similarly, scaling out of a position by taking partial profits at predetermined levels can lock in gains while allowing you to maintain exposure to potential upside.

Risk management is not a static process but an ongoing practice that requires regular review and adjustment. Market conditions change, personal circumstances evolve, and new opportunities and challenges arise. Conduct periodic reviews of your portfolio, strategy, and risk management practices to ensure they remain aligned with your goals and the current market environment. This iterative process is what keeps you resilient, adaptable, and prepared for whatever the market throws your way.

As you integrate these principles and practices into your trading or investing routine, remember that risk management is not about eliminating risk altogether, it's about managing it wisely. The markets are inherently uncertain, and every decision carries some level of risk. By approaching this uncertainty with a clear plan, disciplined execution, and a focus on long-term sustainability, you can turn risk into a tool for growth rather than a source of fear.

Risk management is the foundation that supports all other aspects of market success. Without it, even the most brilliant strategy can falter. With it, you gain the confidence and resilience to navigate challenges, seize opportunities, and stay the course in the face of adversity. Armed with this understanding, you are now ready to explore one of the most critical and challenging aspects of trading: timing the market. In the next chapter, we will delve into the art and science of market timing, equipping you with the tools and techniques to recognize opportunities and avoid common pitfalls.

Chapter 6

TIMING THE MARKET

Timing is one of the most debated and elusive aspects of trading and investing. The ability to recognize when to enter or exit a position can mean the difference between maximizing gains and enduring unnecessary losses. While some argue that market timing is impossible to perfect, there's no denying that a well-timed decision can significantly enhance your overall performance. The art of market timing lies not in achieving perfection but in identifying patterns, signals, and opportunities that improve your odds of success.

At its core, market timing is about understanding the interplay between price movements, market sentiment, and broader economic trends. For traders, this often involves analyzing short-term fluctuations to identify optimal entry and exit points. For long-term investors, timing may focus on capitalizing on broader cycles, such as buying during market corrections or taking profits during speculative bubbles. Regardless of your time horizon, the ability to gauge the market's mood and momentum is a valuable skill.

One of the foundational tools for market timing is technical analysis, which involves studying historical price charts and patterns to predict future movements. Technical analysis operates on the assumption that market behavior is not random but follows discernible trends and cycles. Tools like moving averages, Bollinger Bands, and relative strength index (RSI) help traders identify when prices are overbought, oversold, or approaching critical support and resistance levels. By combining these indicators, you can gain insights into when a trend is likely to continue or reverse.

For example, moving averages provide a smoothed view of price trends, helping you filter out short-term noise. A commonly used strategy is the "golden cross," where a short-term moving average crosses above a long-term moving average, signaling a potential uptrend. Conversely, a "death cross," where the short-term average crosses below the long-term average, may indicate a downturn. While these signals are not foolproof, they can serve as valuable guidelines for timing your trades.

Another approach to market timing is understanding market sentiment. Sentiment indicators measure the overall mood of market participants, offering clues about whether fear, greed, or complacency is driving behavior. Tools like the VIX (Volatility Index), also known as the "fear gauge," provide insights into market uncertainty, while sentiment surveys and put-call ratios can highlight extremes in optimism or pessimism. Extreme sentiment often precedes turning points, as excessive fear or greed creates conditions for reversals.

In addition to technical and sentiment analysis, fundamental factors play a critical role in market timing. Economic indicators such as GDP growth, unemployment rates, and inflation provide a broader context for market movements. For example, rising interest rates may signal a tightening economic environment, which could weigh on equities, while strong corporate earnings might support continued growth in stock prices. Long-term investors often use these indicators to identify undervalued markets or sectors, entering positions during periods of pessimism and exciting when valuations become stretched.

Timing also involves recognizing the impact of external events, such as geopolitical developments, central bank actions, or technological innovations. These events can create sudden shifts in market dynamics, presenting both risks and opportunities. For instance, a central bank's decision to raise interest rates might trigger a sell-off in interest-rate-sensitive assets like bonds or utilities, while a breakthrough in renewable energy technology could spark a rally in clean energy stocks. Staying informed and anticipating how these events might influence the market can give you an edge in timing your decisions.

While timing the market can enhance returns, it also carries risks. Overemphasizing timing can lead to overtrading, where frequent buying and selling erodes profits through transaction costs and taxes. It can also foster a "paralysis by analysis" mindset, where fear of mistiming prevents you from taking action. The key to avoiding these pitfalls is balancing timing with discipline. Rather than trying to catch every market move, focus on high-probability setups that align with your strategy and risk tolerance.

Patience is another critical component of market timing. Impulsive decisions driven by fear of missing out (FOMO) often lead to poor outcomes. For example, buying into a rally at its peak can result in immediate losses if the market reverses. Successful timing requires waiting for confirmation of your analysis, whether it's a technical breakout, a shift in sentiment, or a favorable economic trend. By exercising patience, you increase the likelihood of entering positions at advantageous levels.

For long-term investors, dollar-cost averaging (DCA) offers a practical approach to timing the market without the stress of predicting short-term fluctuations. DCA involves investing a fixed amount of money at regular intervals, regardless of market conditions. This strategy allows you to accumulate assets over time, averaging out your cost basis and reducing the impact of market volatility. While DCA may not capture the absolute lows, it ensures consistent participation in the market, which is often more effective than waiting for the perfect moment.

Even with the best tools and analysis, it's important to acknowledge the limitations of market timing. No one can predict the future with certainty, and even the most sophisticated models are subject to errors and unexpected variables. The goal is not to achieve perfect timing but to improve your decision-making by identifying favorable conditions and avoiding obvious pitfalls. By combining technical, sentiment, and fundamental analysis with discipline and patience, you can navigate the market with greater confidence and consistency.

In the end, timing is a skill that improves with experience. Each decision, whether successful or not, provides valuable insights into market behavior and your own tendencies. Keep a record of your timing decisions, including the rationale behind them and their outcomes. Over time, this practice will help you refine your approach, build confidence, and develop a deeper understanding of the market's rhythms.

As you continue to hone your timing skills, remember that the market rewards those who are prepared, disciplined, and adaptable. Timing is just one piece of the puzzle; it must be integrated with your overall strategy, risk management, and long-term goals. With these elements in place, you'll be well-equipped to seize opportunities and navigate challenges as they arise.

Mastering the art of market timing is as much about psychology and discipline as it is about analysis and tools. While technical, fundamental, and sentimental analysis provide the framework for identifying potential opportunities, the real challenge lies in executing those decisions consistently and without hesitation. The interplay of emotion and timing often separates successful traders from those who struggle to capitalize on opportunities.

One of the most common emotional traps in market timing is the fear of missing out (FOMO). FOMO often strikes during rapidly rising markets or when a particular asset experiences a surge in popularity. Investors driven by FOMO may rush to enter positions without fully analyzing the underlying factors, often buying at or near the peak. This phenomenon was evident during speculative bubbles like the dot-com boom and the cryptocurrency surge of 2017. While the initial euphoria may yield short-term gains, latecomers often find themselves holding overvalued assets as prices correct.

Counteracting FOMO requires a strong commitment to your strategy and a willingness to let opportunities pass if they do not align with your analysis. Remember, the market is not a one-time event but an ongoing cycle. Opportunities will always arise, and exercising patience ensures that you are prepared to act decisively when the conditions align with your plan.

Similarly, fear of loss can paralyze decision-making, causing traders to miss out on opportunities or hesitate when action is required. This fear often manifests during market downturns, when the prospect of further declines creates anxiety about entering or holding positions. To overcome this, it's important to reframe your perspective on losses. Rather than viewing them as failures, they see them as a cost of participating in the market much like a business incurs expenses in pursuit of profits. Effective risk management, including predefined stop-loss orders, can help alleviate this fear by ensuring that losses are controlled and manageable.

Another challenge in timing the market is avoiding the "illusion of control." These cognitive bias leads traders to believe they can predict or influence market outcomes with greater accuracy than is realistically possible. Overconfidence stemming from a string of successful trades can exacerbate this illusion, prompting riskier behavior and larger bets. To guard against overconfidence, adopt a mindset of humility and acknowledge the role of uncertainty in the market. Even the most informed decisions carry an element of chance, and maintaining this awareness fosters a balanced and objective approach.

One technique that can help traders stay grounded is setting clear criteria for entering and exiting positions. These criteria should be based on your strategy and supported by analysis, whether it's a specific price pattern, technical signal, or fundamental event. By defining your rules in advance, you reduce the influence of emotions and ensure that your decisions are consistent and rational. For instance, a trader using a breakout strategy might enter a position only when a stock closes above a key resistance level with strong volume, while an investor focusing on value might buy only when a company's P/E ratio falls below a certain threshold.

Practicing selective timing is another way to enhance your performance. The goal is not to act on every signal but to focus on high-probability opportunities that offer a favorable risk-to-reward ratio. Selectivity requires discipline and a willingness to wait for the right conditions, even if it means sitting out of the market during uncertain periods. This approach contrasts with overtrading, which not only increases transaction costs but also exposes you to unnecessary risks. By prioritizing quality over quantity, you can improve the overall efficiency of your timing decisions.

Another advanced concept in market timing is the use of intermarket analysis. Intermarket analysis examines the relationships between different asset classes, such as stocks, bonds, commodities, and currencies, to identify trends and correlations. For example, a rising U.S. dollar might signal weakness in commodities priced in dollars, such as gold or oil. Similarly, declining bond yields could indicate lower borrowing costs and support equity markets. Understanding these relationships provides a broader context for your timing decisions, helping you anticipate market shifts before they become apparent in individual asset prices.

The role of macroeconomic cycles cannot be overlooked when it comes to timing the market. Economic indicators like unemployment rates, consumer confidence, and manufacturing data offer valuable insights into the health of the economy and its potential impact on asset prices. For example, during periods of economic expansion, consumer discretionary stocks may outperform as spending increases, while defensive sectors like utilities and healthcare may gain favor during recessions. Recognizing these cycles and aligning your timing decisions with the prevailing economic environment can give you an edge.

While timing the market is often associated with active trading, it also plays a role in long-term investing. For instance, value investors often seek to buy assets during market downturns, when fear and pessimism drive prices below their intrinsic value. This approach requires patience, as it may take time for market sentiment to recover and prices to rebound. Similarly, long-term investors may choose to reduce exposure during speculative bubbles, locking in gains and preserving capital for future opportunities.

It's important to emphasize that market timing is not about predicting the future but about responding to opportunities and risks as they arise. No one can consistently forecast market movements with precision, and attempting to do so often leads to frustration and poor decision-making. Instead, focus on building a framework that helps you identify favorable conditions, manage risks, and execute decisions with confidence. This framework should be rooted in analysis, supported by tools, and guided by discipline.

Timing the market is both an art and a science, blending technical expertise with emotional resilience and strategic thinking. As you refined your skills, remember that perfection is neither possible nor necessary. The goal is to improve incrementally, learning from each experience and building a stronger foundation for future success.

With a deeper understanding of market timing, you are now equipped to take your trading and investing to the next level. In the following chapter, we will explore how to build a resilient portfolio, one that balances risk and return while adapting to changing market conditions. This is where strategy and execution come together to create a sustainable path to financial success.

Chapter 7

BUILDING A RESILIENT PORTFOLIO

A Resilient portfolio is the backbone of long-term financial success. While individual trades or investments may capture attention and generate short-term returns, it's the structure and composition of your overall portfolio that determine your ability to weather market turbulence and achieve sustainable growth. Building a portfolio that balances risk and return requires careful planning, ongoing management, and an understanding of how to adapt to changing market conditions.

At the core of portfolio construction is the principle of diversification. Diversification reduces risk by spreading investments across different asset classes, sectors, and geographic regions. The rationale is straightforward: when one area of the market underperforms, gains in other areas can offset losses, smoothing out overall returns. For example, a portfolio that includes both stocks and bonds may perform better during a market downturn than one concentrated solely in equities, as bonds often act as a safe haven during periods of volatility.

Diversification extends beyond simply holding a variety of assets. True diversification requires considering correlations between assets, the extent to which their prices move in relation to each other. For instance, adding two stocks from the same sector, such as technology, may not significantly reduce risk because they are likely to be affected by the same market forces. On the other hand, combining assets with low or negative correlations, such as stocks and commodities, can enhance portfolio resilience by reducing exposure to sector-specific risks.

One of the most effective tools for achieving diversification is asset allocation. Asset allocation refers to the process of dividing your portfolio among different asset classes, such as equities, fixed income, real estate, and cash. The optimal allocation depends on your financial goals, risk tolerance, and investment horizon. Younger investors with a long-time horizon may allocate a larger portion of their portfolio to equities, which offer higher growth potential but greater volatility. Conversely, retirees or those nearing retirement might favor a more conservative allocation, prioritizing income and capital preservation through bonds or dividend-paying stocks.

Strategic asset allocation involves setting target percentages for each asset class and rebalancing periodically to maintain those targets. For example, if your target allocation is 60% equities and 40% bonds, and a strong equity market rally increases the equity portion to 70%, you would sell some stocks and buy bonds to return to your original allocation. This disciplined approach helps you avoid the temptation to chase performance and ensures that your portfolio remains aligned with your risk tolerance and objectives.

Tactical asset allocation takes a more dynamic approach, allowing for adjustments based on market conditions or economic outlook. For instance, during a period of rising interest rates, you might reduce exposure to rate-sensitive bonds and increase allocations to sectors like financials that tend to benefit from higher rates. While tactical allocation can enhance returns, it requires a deeper understanding of market trends and carries the risk of mistiming shifts.

Sector and industry diversification add another layer of resilience to your portfolio. Within the equity portion of your portfolio, consider spreading investments across different sectors, such as technology, healthcare, consumer goods, and energy. Each sector responds differently to economic cycles, geopolitical events, and technological advancements, so a balanced mix can reduce the impact of sector-specific downturns. For example, while the technology sector may struggle during a period of rising interest rates, the healthcare sector may remain stable due to consistent demand for medical services.

Geographic diversification is equally important in today's globalized economy. Investing in international markets can provide exposure to growth opportunities and reduce dependence on the performance of a single country or region. For instance, adding emerging market equities to a predominantly U.S.-based portfolio can enhance returns during periods of global economic expansion. However, international investing also introduces risks such as currency fluctuations and geopolitical instability, so it's important to weigh these factors when considering global diversification.

Another consideration in building a resilient portfolio is the role of alternative investments. Alternatives include assets like real estate, commodities, private equity, and hedge funds. These investments often have lower correlations with traditional asset classes, providing additional diversification benefits. For example, real estate can generate income through rental yields while offering protection against inflation, as property values tend to rise with the cost of living. Commodities like gold or oil can act as hedges against market volatility or geopolitical risks. However, alternatives often come with higher fees, lower liquidity, and greater complexity, so they should be used selectively and in proportion to your overall strategy.

Managing risk at the portfolio level requires regular monitoring and adjustments. Market conditions, economic trends, and personal circumstances can all influence the performance of your investments and the appropriateness of your allocation. Periodic reviews, typically conducted annually or semi-annually, allow you to assess whether your portfolio is still aligned with your goals and risk tolerance. Rebalancing during these reviews ensures that your allocation remains on track, preventing any single asset class or sector from dominating your portfolio.

Behavioral discipline is crucial in portfolio management. Emotional reactions to market movements can lead to impulsive decisions, such as selling during downturns or chasing returns during rallies. A well-defined portfolio strategy provides a framework for staying the course during periods of volatility, helping you avoid costly mistakes. For example, during a market correction, disciplined investors with diversified portfolios are more likely to remain invested, taking advantage of lower prices to rebalance and position themselves for future recovery.

Building a resilient portfolio also means considering your long-term financial plan. Your portfolio is just one component of your broader financial picture, which includes factors like income, expenses, debt, and retirement goals. Integrating your portfolio strategy with your overall financial plan ensures that your investments are working toward your ultimate objectives, whether that's funding a comfortable retirement, supporting your family, or achieving financial independence.

Finally, resilience in portfolio management is not just about avoiding losses but also about capturing opportunities. By maintaining a disciplined approach, staying diversified, and adapting to changes in the market, you position yourself to take advantage of growth potential while mitigating risks.

A resilient portfolio provides the confidence and stability needed to navigate the ups and downs of the market, enabling you to stay focused on your long-term goals.

A resilient portfolio is not only a safeguard against market turbulence but also a dynamic tool for seizing opportunities across different economic environments. As markets evolve, your portfolio must remain flexible and adaptable, capable of responding to shifting trends without compromising its foundational principles. This balance between stability and adaptability is what transforms a good portfolio into a resilient one.

An often-overlooked aspect of portfolio resilience is liquidity. Liquidity refers to how quickly and easily an asset can be converted into cash without significantly affecting its price. Highly liquid assets, such as large-cap stocks and government bonds, can be bought or sold almost instantly. Illiquid assets, like real estate or private equity, may take weeks, months, or even years to sell. While illiquid assets can provide diversification and unique growth opportunities, holding too large a portion of your portfolio in illiquid investments can leave you vulnerable during times of financial stress or unexpected expenses. A balanced portfolio should include a mix of liquid and illiquid assets, ensuring that you have access to cash when needed.

Inflation protection is another critical consideration. Inflation erodes the purchasing power of money, which can diminish the real returns on investments. Certain asset classes, such as equities, real estate, and commodities, tend to perform well during inflationary periods because they have the potential to increase in value along with rising prices. Treasury Inflation-Protected Securities (TIPS) are another option for safeguarding against inflation, as their principal value adjusts with inflation rates. Including inflation-resistant assets in your portfolio ensures that your purchasing power is preserved over time.

Tax efficiency is equally important in building a resilient portfolio. Taxes can significantly impact your investment returns, particularly over the long term. Understanding the tax implications of different investments and account types is crucial. For example, holding income-generating assets like bonds in tax-advantaged accounts such as IRAs or 401(k)s can help reduce your tax liability. Similarly, capital gains taxes can be minimized by holding investments for more than a year to qualify for long-term capital gains rates. Leveraging tax-efficient funds, such as index funds and

ETFs, which typically have lower turnover rates, can further enhance after-tax returns.

One of the most powerful tools for long-term portfolio resilience is compounding. Compounding occurs when the returns on your investments generate additional returns over time. For compounding to work effectively, two factors are essential: reinvestment and time. Reinvesting dividends, interest, and capital gains allows your portfolio to grow exponentially, while a longer investment horizon magnifies the compounding effect. This is why starting early and maintaining a disciplined approach are critical to building wealth over the long term.

Behavioral factors also play a significant role in portfolio resilience. Even the most carefully constructed portfolio can falter if emotional reactions lead to poor decision-making. Fear, greed, and impatience are common culprits that can derail long-term plans. For instance, selling during a market downturn out of fear of further losses may lock in losses and prevent you from participating in the subsequent recovery. Conversely, chasing high-flying investments during speculative bubbles often leads to buying at inflated prices and suffering losses when the bubble bursts. The key to overcoming these emotional pitfalls is maintaining a long-term perspective and adhering to your strategy, even in the face of short-term volatility.

Scenario planning is another advanced technique for enhancing portfolio resilience. This involves considering potential future events and their impact on your portfolio, such as economic recessions, interest rate hikes, or technological disruptions. By analyzing how your portfolio might perform under different scenarios, you can identify vulnerabilities and take proactive steps to address them. For example, if a scenario analysis reveals that your portfolio is heavily exposed to rising interest rates, you might consider reducing your allocation to long-duration bonds or increasing exposure to rate-sensitive sectors like financials.

Risk-adjusted returns are a critical metric for evaluating portfolio performance. Rather than focusing solely on absolute returns, risk-adjusted measures like the Sharpe ratio and the Sortino ratio assess how much risk you are taking to achieve your returns. A portfolio with a high risk-adjusted return delivers strong performance while minimizing volatility, which is the hallmark of resilience. Regularly reviewing your portfolio's risk-adjusted performance helps ensure that you are being adequately compensated for the risks you are taking.

Incorporating sustainable and socially responsible investments (SRI) can also add a layer of resilience to your portfolio. Companies with strong environmental, social, and governance (ESG) practices often demonstrate better risk management, operational efficiency, and long-term growth potential. While ESG investing has traditionally been viewed as a values-based approach, it is increasingly recognized as a way to identify resilient companies that are well-positioned to navigate global challenges such as climate change, regulatory shifts, and evolving consumer preferences.

Technology and automation are transforming portfolio management, making it easier to build and maintain resilience. Robo-advisors, for example, use algorithms to create and manage diversified portfolios based on your risk tolerance and financial goals. These platforms offer low-cost, hands-off solutions for investors who want to maintain a resilient portfolio without the complexity of manual management. Additionally, portfolio management software and apps provide tools for tracking performance, analyzing diversification, and rebalancing automatically, ensuring that your portfolio remains aligned with your objectives.

As you refine your approach to portfolio construction, remember that resilience is an ongoing process. Market conditions, economic environments, and personal circumstances are constantly evolving, and your portfolio must evolve with them. Regular reviews, disciplined adjustments, and a commitment to your long-term goals are the keys to maintaining resilience and achieving sustainable success.

Chapter 8

ADVANCE TRADING TECHNIQUES

As your market experience deepens, you may find yourself seeking ways to expand your toolkit, diversify your strategies, and potentially enhance returns. Advanced trading techniques such as derivatives trading, hedging, and algorithmic strategies offer new avenues for growth, but they also come with heightened complexity and risk. Mastering these techniques requires a solid foundation in market fundamentals, a clear understanding of your goals, and the discipline to manage risks effectively.

One of the most versatile tools in advanced trading is the use of **derivatives**. Derivatives are financial instruments whose value is derived from an underlying asset, such as a stock, bond, commodity, or currency. Common types of derivatives include options, futures, swaps, and forwards. These instruments allow traders to speculate on price movements, hedge against risk, and gain exposure to markets with minimal upfront capital. However, their complexity and leverage can amplify both gains and losses, making them unsuitable for beginners or those without a well-defined strategy.

Options trading is one of the most popular forms of derivatives trading. Options give the holder the right, but not the obligation, to buy or sell an underlying asset at a specified price within a certain timeframe. There are two main types of options: calls and puts. A call option provides the right to buy an asset, while a put option provides the right to sell it. Options can be used to speculate on market direction, hedge existing positions, or generate income through strategies like covered calls or cash-secured puts.

For example, suppose your own shares of a stock that you believe may decline in the short term but remain strong in the long term. You could purchase a put option to protect against potential losses, effectively setting a floor for how much you could lose on the position. On the other hand, if you expect a stock to rise but want to limit your initial investment, you could buy a call option, which allows you to benefit from the upside while risking only the premium paid for the option.

Another widely used derivative is the futures contract. Futures are agreements to buy or sell an asset at a predetermined price on a specified date. They are commonly used in commodities markets to hedge against price fluctuations or speculate on future price movements. For instance, a farmer might use futures to lock in a price for their crop, ensuring profitability regardless of market volatility. Futures contracts are also popular among traders seeking leveraged exposure to indices, currencies, or interest rates.

While options and futures can be powerful tools, they require careful risk management. The leverage inherent in derivatives means that small market movements can result in outsized gains or losses. To mitigate these risks, traders often use stop-loss orders, position sizing rules, and strategies that cap potential losses, such as spreads or collars. A thorough understanding of pricing models, such as the Black-Scholes formula for options, is also essential for making informed decisions.

Hedging is another advanced technique that can enhance portfolio resilience while managing risk. Hedging involves taking offsetting positions to protect against adverse market movements. For example, an investor holding a portfolio of technology stocks might use index options or futures to hedge against a broader market downturn. Similarly, a business exposed to foreign currency risk might use forward contracts to lock in exchange rates and mitigate potential losses.

While hedging can reduce risk, it is not without costs. Derivative premiums, transaction fees, and opportunity costs can erode returns, so hedging strategies should be used judiciously and aligned with your overall objectives. The goal of hedging is not to eliminate risk entirely but to balance risk and reward in a way that supports your financial goals.

Algorithmic trading is another area of advanced trading that has gained prominence in recent years. Algorithmic trading, or "algo trading," involves using computer programs to execute trades based on predefined criteria, such as price, volume, or technical indicators. Algorithms can be designed for a wide range of strategies, from high-frequency trading (HFT) to arbitrage, momentum trading, and market making.

One of the primary advantages of algorithmic trading is its ability to eliminate emotional biases and execute trades with speed and precision. For example, a trend-following algorithm might automatically buy when a stock price crosses above its 50-day moving average and sell when it drops below. By removing human judgment from the equation, algorithms can enhance consistency and reduce the impact of psychological factors such as fear and greed.

However, developing and deploying algorithms requires technical expertise, including programming skills and a deep understanding of market mechanics. Back testing is a critical step in algorithm development, allowing you to evaluate how the strategy would have performed under historical market conditions. Forward testing in live or simulated environments helps ensure that the algorithm behaves as expected in real-time markets.

Leveraged products, such as CFDs (Contracts for Difference) and leveraged ETFs, offer another avenue for advanced traders. These products amplify exposure to an underlying asset, enabling traders to control a larger position with a smaller initial investment. While leverage can magnify returns, it also increases the risk of significant losses, making it essential to use these instruments with caution and a clear risk management plan.

Finally, advanced trading techniques often involve a combination of strategies tailored to specific market conditions. For example, during periods of low volatility, traders might focus on income-generating strategies like selling options (e.g., covered calls or cash-secured puts). In contrast, during periods of heightened volatility, strategies that benefit from price swings, such as straddles or strangles, may be more appropriate. The ability to adapt your approach based on the market environment is a hallmark of advanced trading.

While advanced trading techniques can unlock new opportunities, they are not without risks. Success in this realm requires continuous learning, disciplined execution, and a willingness to adapt. As you incorporate these techniques into your toolkit, start small, focus on mastering one strategy at a time, and never risk more than you can afford to lose.

Advanced trading techniques open a world of possibilities, allowing you to capitalize on market movements with precision and creativity. However, these strategies require a deep understanding of financial instruments, disciplined execution, and a focus on risk management. While they can enhance your trading arsenal, they also introduce complexities and risks that demand careful study and practice.

One of the most versatile tools in advanced trading is the use of options. These derivatives provide the flexibility to profit in any market condition rising, falling, or sideways. Beyond simple call and options, traders often employ multi-leg strategies to refine their risk-reward profiles. For instance, a spread strategy, such as a bull call spread, involves buying a call option at a lower strike price while selling another at a higher strike price. This reduces the cost of the trade but caps potential profits. In contrast, a straddle involves purchasing both a call and a put at the same strike price, making it a popular choice in highly volatile markets. Each of these strategies requires a nuanced understanding of market conditions, as well as precise execution to balance potential gains and risks.

Futures contracts offer another powerful avenue for advanced traders. These standardized agreements allow you to buy or sell an asset at a predetermined price on a specified date. Futures are commonly used in commodities trading but are equally effective in hedging or speculating in equities, currencies, and interest rates. For example, a farmer might sell grain futures to lock in a price for their crop, protecting against the risk of a price decline. On the speculative side, a trader might use oil futures to profit from anticipated changes in energy prices. While futures offer leverage and flexibility, their potential for significant losses demands rigorous risk management and a clear understanding of margin requirements.

Hedging is a core strategy in advanced trading, providing a means to protect your portfolio against adverse market movements. By taking offsetting positions, you can reduce the impact of losses in one area of your portfolio. For instance, an investor who is heavily invested in technology stocks might buy options on a tech index to mitigate the risk of a sector-wide downturn. Similarly, a global investor might use currency forward contracts to hedge against unfavorable exchange rate fluctuations. While hedging comes with costs, such as option premiums or transaction fees, it can be invaluable for preserving capital and maintaining stability during volatile periods.

The advent of algorithmic trading has revolutionized the financial markets, offering traders a way to automate their strategies and eliminate emotional biases. Algorithms can execute trades based on predefined criteria, such as price levels, technical indicators, or market conditions. Momentum algorithms, for example, buy when prices are rising and sell when they begin to fall, capitalizing on trends. Mean-reversion strategies, on the other hand, seek to profit from assets that deviate significantly from their historical averages. While algorithms offer speed and precision, they require technical expertise in programming and a thorough understanding of back testing and optimization to ensure they perform as intended.

Leveraged instruments, such as contracts for difference (CFDs) and leveraged ETFs, enable traders to amplify their exposure to an asset without requiring significant upfront capital. For example, a 2x leveraged ETF aims to deliver double the daily return of its underlying index. While these products can magnify gains, they also increase the risk of substantial losses, particularly over extended periods due to compounding effects. As such, they are best suited for short-term strategies and require careful monitoring.

Advanced trading techniques also include strategies tailored to specific market conditions. During periods of low volatility, traders might employ income-generating strategies like selling covered calls, where they own the underlying stock and sell call options to earn premiums. In contrast, during heightened volatility, strategies like strangles or straddles, which involve buying options to profit from large price swings, may be more effective. The ability to adapt your approach based on the prevailing environment is critical to leveraging advanced techniques successfully.

While these strategies hold great potential, they are not without risk. Their complexity demands continuous learning and disciplined execution. Success in advanced trading requires a methodical approach: start with a single strategy, master it, and gradually incorporate additional techniques as your confidence and understanding grow. Regularly reviewing and refining your methods ensures they remain effective in the face of evolving market conditions.

Advanced trading is not about chasing quick wins but about expanding your toolkit to navigate diverse market scenarios with confidence. By integrating options, futures, hedging, and algorithmic strategies into your trading plan, you can unlock new opportunities and enhance your overall performance. However, the foundational principles of discipline, risk management, and continuous learning remain as vital as ever. With these principles guiding your approach, you are better equipped to succeed in the complex and dynamic world of advanced trading.

Chapter 9

LEARNING FROM THE GREATS

Every great trader and investor have a story. Behind their success are lessons learned through triumphs, failures, and the relentless pursuit of mastery. While no two market journeys are alike, the principles and strategies employed by the most successful investors often share common themes: discipline, patience, adaptability, and a deep understanding of market dynamics. By studying their experiences, we gain invaluable insights that can inform and inspire our own market journeys.

Perhaps no figure is as synonymous with investing success as **Warren Buffett**, often referred to as the "Oracle of Omaha." Buffett's approach is rooted in value investing, a strategy that seeks to buy stocks at prices below their intrinsic value. Guided by the principles of his mentor, Benjamin Graham, Buffett looks for companies with strong fundamentals, competitive advantages, and consistent earnings. He is famously patient, often holding investments for decades, allowing the power of compounding to work in his favor. Buffett's emphasis on understanding the businesses he invests in, rather than speculating on short-term price movements, underscores the importance of research and conviction in successful investing.

Buffett's career also highlights the value of staying calm during market downturns. When others panic, Buffett often seizes opportunities, famously stating, "Be fearful when others are greedy, and greedy when others are fearful." This contrarian mindset has enabled him to capitalize on undervalued opportunities during times of market distress, reinforcing the importance of maintaining a long-term perspective and resisting emotional decision-making.

Another legendary figure, **George Soros**, offers a starkly different approach to market success. Known as the "man who broke the Bank of England," Soros built his fortune through speculative trading and macroeconomic analysis. His most famous trade, shorting the British pound in 1992, earned him over $1 billion in a single day. Soros's philosophy centers on identifying large-scale economic imbalances and positioning himself to profit from their eventual correction. He places a strong emphasis on flexibility, often reassessing and reversing his positions as new information emerges.

Soros's approach demonstrates the importance of intellectual humility. Unlike many traders who cling to their beliefs, Soros embraces uncertainty and adjusts his strategies accordingly. His ability to pivot quickly and decisively is a testament to the value of adaptability in a dynamic market environment. Soros also emphasizes the concept of reflexivity, the idea that market participants' perceptions and actions influence market outcomes, creating feedback loops that can amplify trends or reversals.

Jesse Livermore, often regarded as one of the greatest traders of all time, provides timeless lessons on speculation and risk management. Operating in the early 20th century, Livermore made and lost several fortunes by trading stocks and commodities. His book, *Reminiscences of a Stock Operator*, remains a classic, offering insights into the psychology of trading and the importance of timing. Livermore was a master of trend following, often waiting for confirmation before entering a trade. He understood that markets move in cycles and that patience is often rewarded.

Livermore's story also serves as a cautionary tale about the dangers of overleveraging and emotional trading. Despite his immense skill, he suffered significant losses due to a lack of discipline in risk management. His experiences highlight the importance of setting clear rules, sticking to them, and avoiding the temptation to chase losses.

The modern era has introduced a new breed of market legends, including **Ray Dalio**, the founder of Bridgewater Associates, one of the world's largest hedge funds. Dalio's approach, known as "radical transparency," emphasizes data-driven decision-making and rigorous analysis. His *All-Weather* portfolio strategy, designed to perform well across different economic environments, reflects his deep understanding of macroeconomic cycles. Dalio's emphasis on diversification and risk parity underscores the importance of balancing risk and reward in portfolio construction.

Dalio's career also demonstrates the value of learning from mistakes. His early missteps, including a high-profile prediction that failed to materialize, taught him the importance of humility and adaptability. Dalio often refers to his mistakes as "painful failures that turned into principles," emphasizing the role of continuous learning in achieving long-term success.

Another key figure in modern investing is **Cathie Wood**, the founder of ARK Invest. Wood is known for her focus on disruptive innovation, investing in cutting-edge sectors like biotechnology, artificial intelligence, and renewable energy. Her approach underscores the importance of identifying long-term trends and being willing to take calculated risks on emerging technologies. While her strategies have faced criticism during periods of underperformance, Wood's conviction and ability to articulate her vision have made her a prominent figure in the investing world.

The lessons from these greats are not limited to specific strategies or market conditions. They highlight universal principles that transcend individual trades or investments. Discipline, patience, and adaptability are recurring themes, as is the ability to maintain a clear focus on long-term goals. The importance of continuous learning, intellectual humility, and effective risk management cannot be overstated.

Studying the experiences of legendary investors and traders is not about copying their methods but about understanding their principles and applying them to your unique circumstances. Each of these figures faced challenges, made mistakes, and adapted their approaches over time. Their stories serve as a reminder that success in the market is a journey, not a destination, and that perseverance, resilience, and a commitment to growth are the keys to lasting achievement.

As you reflect on the lessons of the greats, consider how their experiences can inform you of your own approach. Are you disciplined in your decision-making? Do you maintain a long-term perspective? Are you willing to adapt when circumstances change? By integrating these principles into your strategy, you position yourself to navigate the complexities of the market with confidence and clarity.

The stories of legendary investors and traders are as much about perseverance and resilience as they are about financial acumen. Their successes were built on a foundation of hard-earned lessons, often learned through failure and recovery. These experiences provide a treasure trove of insights, helping us understand the mindsets and strategies that lead to sustained success in the market.

Take the story of **Paul Tudor Jones**, a hedge fund manager renowned for his ability to predict and profit from market crashes. Jones's defining moment came in 1987 when he famously anticipated the Black Monday stock market crash. Using technical analysis and a deep understanding of historical market patterns, he shorted the market and achieved staggering returns while others faced devastating losses. Jones's approach underscores the importance of preparation and adaptability. He recognized the warning signs of an overheated market and positioned himself, accordingly, demonstrating the value of staying informed and acting decisively when opportunities arise.

Jones is also a staunch advocate of risk management. He adheres to a principle he calls "losers' average losers," which warns against the tendency to double down on losing positions in an attempt to recover losses. This discipline has been instrumental in his long-term success, ensuring that no single mistake undermines his broader goals. His story serves as a reminder that protecting capital is just as important as seeking profits and that the ability to manage risk effectively is a hallmark of great traders.

Peter Lynch, the legendary manager of the Fidelity Magellan Fund, offers another perspective on market success. Lynch's investment philosophy, often summarized as "invest in what you know," emphasizes the value of understanding the companies and industries in which you invest. He believed that individual investors have an edge in identifying opportunities within their own areas of expertise, whether it's a new product they love or a trend they observe in their professional lives.

During his tenure at Magellan, Lynch delivered an average annual return of 29.2%, significantly outperforming the market. His strategy focused on identifying undervalued growth stocks, often referred to as "ten baggers" companies whose stock price increased tenfold or more. Lynch's ability to spot these opportunities stemmed from his meticulous research, hands-on approach, and willingness to think independently. His success highlights the importance of curiosity, due diligence, and a willingness to act on your convictions.

The career of **Stanley Druckenmiller**, a protégé of George Soros, is another masterclass in adaptability and timing. Druckenmiller is known for his ability to deliver consistent returns across different market environments. His investment style combines macroeconomic analysis with a willingness to take large, concentrated positions when he sees a high-probability opportunity. Druckenmiller's philosophy of "keeping the ball moving" reflects his focus on avoiding unnecessary risks while maintaining consistent progress. His career is a testament to the importance of balancing boldness with caution and knowing when to pivot as market conditions change.

One of the most intriguing aspects of Druckenmiller's success is his emphasis on simplicity. Despite managing billions of dollars, he avoids overcomplicating his strategies, instead focusing on clear, actionable insights. He once remarked, "It's not about whether you're right or wrong. It's about how much money you make when you're right and how much you lose when you're wrong. This principle highlights the importance of risk-reward analysis and underscores the need to let winners run while cutting losses quickly.

Ed Seykota, a pioneer of computerized trading systems, offers valuable lessons on the psychological aspects of trading. Seykota's career is notable for his early adoption of algorithmic trading, which allowed him to remove emotional biases from his decisions. His results were extraordinary, with one of his managed accounts achieving returns of over 250,000% during a multi-decade period. Seykota's approach emphasizes the importance of discipline, systematic execution, and a long-term perspective.

In his book *The Trading Tribe*, Seykota delves into the emotional challenges traders face, such as fear, greed, and overconfidence. He argues that personal growth and emotional awareness are just as important as technical skills in achieving success. Seykota's story underscores the importance of developing a mindset that supports consistency and resilience, particularly during periods of market turbulence.

The lessons from these market legends extend beyond their specific strategies or achievements. They demonstrate the importance of adaptability in a constantly changing environment, the value of continuous learning, and the necessity of staying disciplined in the face of uncertainty. Their stories also highlight the diverse paths to success, from Buffett's patient, value-driven approach to Soros's bold, macroeconomic bets.

Studying these figures also reveals the importance of context. Each investor and trader operated in a unique market environment, shaped by the economic, technological, and geopolitical forces of their time. For instance, Livermore's success was tied to the unregulated, often chaotic markets of the early 20th century, while Dalio's strategies reflect the data-driven, globally interconnected nature of modern finance. Understanding the context in which these legends operated helps us extract principles that remain relevant while adapting their lessons to today's market landscape.

In addition to studying their successes, it's equally important to learn from their failures. Nearly every market legend has faced setbacks, whether it's Livermore's repeated bankruptcies, Soros's incorrect predictions, or Dalio's early mistakes. These failures reveal the importance of humility, the need for robust risk management, and the value of perseverance. They remind us that success in the market is not about avoiding mistakes altogether but about learning from them and growing stronger as a result.

The common thread among these greats is their commitment to growth; both as investors and as individuals. They view the market not just as a place to make money but as a platform for testing ideas, refining strategies, and building resilience. Their stories inspire us to embrace the challenges of the market with curiosity, determination, and a willingness to learn.

As you reflect on the lessons from these legends, consider how their principles can guide your own journey. Are you disciplined in your approach? Do you adapt to changing conditions? Are you committed to continuous learning? By integrating these qualities into your strategy, you position yourself to navigate the complexities of the market and achieve sustained success.

With these timeless insights in mind, we turn to the final chapter of this journey: sustaining success over the long term. In the next chapter, we will explore how to maintain focus, avoid burnout, and ensure that your market achievements align with your broader life goals.

The most valuable lessons from market legends are not just about their successes but the mindsets, habits, and principles that sustained them over decades. Their stories provide a roadmap for navigating the markets with purpose, discipline, and resilience. By delving deeper into their philosophies and examining how they approached challenges, we can extract powerful insights that apply to traders and investors of all levels.

Howard Marks, co-founder of Oaktree Capital Management, is a Master of Risk assessment and value investing. Marks emphasizes the importance of understanding cycles, economics, market, and emotional and positioning oneself accordingly. In his book *The Most Important Thing*, he discusses the concept of "second-level thinking," which involves going beyond surface-level analysis to anticipate how others will react to market developments. For example, when the market is euphoric, second-level thinking might lead you to act cautiously, anticipating a correction.

Marks also teaches the importance of controlling what you can. He recognizes that while markets are inherently unpredictable, disciplined risk management and a focus on intrinsic value can help investors avoid costly mistakes. His approach highlights the value of patience and a long-term perspective, especially during times of market volatility or uncertainty. By staying focused on fundamentals and ignoring the noise of short-term fluctuations, Marks has consistently delivered strong returns for his investors.

Another influential figure, **Charlie Munger**, Warren Buffett's long-time partner at Berkshire Hathaway, complements Buffett's value investing philosophy with his multidisciplinary approach to decision-making. Munger is a firm believer in mental models' frameworks for understanding the world and making better decisions. He draws on principles from disciplines like psychology, economics, and biology to analyze investments and anticipate market behavior. Munger's advice to "invert, always invert" encourages looking at problems from multiple angles, such as considering what actions to avoid as much as what actions to take.

Munger's wit and wisdom are encapsulated in his famous admonition to "be a learning machine." He stresses the importance of lifelong learning and intellectual humility, urging investors to continuously expand their knowledge and adapt to changing conditions. Munger's ability to synthesize insights from diverse fields underscores the value of broad thinking in navigating complex markets.

The lessons of **John Bogle**, the founder of Vanguard and the pioneer of index investing, offer a different perspective. Bogle's advocacy for low-cost, passive investing transformed the financial industry and empowered millions of individual investors. He championed the idea that "costs matter," emphasizing that high fees and frequent trading can erode returns over time. His creation of the first index fund provided a simple, low-cost way for investors to achieve market returns without the risks and complexities of active management.

Bogle's approach is rooted in simplicity and patience. He believed that attempting to time the market or outperform benchmarks often leads to subpar results due to human error and overconfidence. His advice to "stay the course" resonates as a reminder to focus on long-term goals and avoid being swayed by short-term market noise. Bogle's legacy highlights the power of disciplined, low-cost investing as a means to build wealth sustainably.

Anne Scheiber, a lesser known but equally inspiring figure, exemplifies the power of long-term investing and compounding. Starting with a modest sum, Scheiber built a portfolio worth over $22 million by the time of her death. She achieved this through a combination of patience, frugality, and an unwavering focus on dividend-paying stocks. Scheiber reinvested her dividends and avoided unnecessary trading, allowing compounding to work its magic over decades.

Her story is a testament to the fact that market success is not limited to professionals or those with large sums of money. By sticking to a simple, consistent strategy and resisting the urge to chase trends, Scheiber demonstrated that anyone with discipline and a long-term mindset can achieve extraordinary results.

The lessons from these greats extend beyond the technical aspects of investing. They also highlight the importance of emotional resilience. Markets are inherently volatile, and the ability to stay composed during periods of uncertainty or downturns is a defining trait of successful investors. For example, during the 2008 financial crisis, many investors panicked and sold their holdings at steep losses. Those who maintained a long-term perspective, however, were rewarded as markets recovered and eventually reached new highs.

Resilience also involves learning to embrace failure. Nearly every legendary investor has faced setbacks, whether it's a failed trade, a misjudged market, or a broader economic crisis. What sets them apart is their ability to reflect on these experiences, extract lessons, and improve. Soros famously said, "It's not whether you're right or wrong that matters, but how much money you make when you're right and how much you lose when you're wrong." This perspective underscores the importance of managing losses and focusing on overall performance rather than individual outcomes.

The greats also teach us the importance of conviction. Whether it's Buffett's commitment to buying quality businesses at fair prices or Bogle's belief in the power of indexing, their success stems from their willingness to stick to their principles even when faced with skepticism or criticism. Conviction is not about stubbornness; it's about having the confidence to act on your analysis and the patience to see it through.

Chapter 10

THE LONG GAME

Achieving success in the financial markets is a significant milestone but sustaining that success over the long term is an entirely different challenge. The market is a dynamic and unpredictable environment, and even the most skilled traders and investors can falter without a long-term perspective. Beyond strategies, tools, and techniques, lasting success in the market requires resilience, adaptability, and a commitment to personal and professional growth. It also involves aligning your market achievements with your broader life goals, ensuring that financial success supports a fulfilling and meaningful life.

One of the most important aspects of playing the long game is the ability to stay disciplined through the inevitable ups and downs of the market. Success breeds confidence, but it can also lead to complacency or overconfidence. Traders who experience a string of wins may begin to take excessive risk, believing they are immune to losses. Conversely, a series of setbacks can erode confidence and lead to impulsive decision-making. The key to avoiding these pitfalls is maintaining a consistent approach, rooted in your principles and objectives, regardless of short-term results.

A long-term perspective also involves focusing on incremental progress rather than chasing quick wins. Compounding is a powerful force, and the rewards of steady, consistent growth far outweigh the fleeting gains of speculative bets. For instance, an investor who achieves an average annual return of 10% over 20 years will see their portfolio grow more than sixfold. This exponential growth is only possible with patience, discipline, and a commitment to reinvesting earnings.

Another critical factor in sustaining success is managing burnout. The intensity of trading and investing, coupled with the constant flow of information and the emotional highs and lows of market movements, can take a toll on mental and physical well-being. To avoid burnout, it's important to set boundaries and prioritize self-care. This might include limiting the time spent monitoring markets, taking regular breaks, and engaging in activities that provide relaxation and balance.

Maintaining a balanced life is not just about preserving your energy, it also enhances your decision-making. A clear and rested mind is better equipped to process information, identify opportunities, and make rational decisions. Many successful investors, from Buffett to Dalio, emphasize the importance of maintaining perspective and avoiding emotional reactions. By cultivating habits that support mental clarity and emotional stability, you can approach the market with greater focus and confidence.

Adaptability is another hallmark of long-term success. Markets evolve, and strategies that work in one environment may become obsolete in another. For example, the rise of algorithmic trading and passive investing has fundamentally changed the dynamics of many markets, making it harder for traditional stock-picking strategies to outperform. Staying informed about trends, technologies, and innovations is essential for remaining competitive. This might involve learning new skills, such as programming for algorithmic trading, or exploring emerging markets and asset classes.

Continuous learning is not just a necessity but a mindset. The best traders and investors view the market as a never-ending journey of discovery, where each experience whether a success or failure is an opportunity to grow. Reading books, attending seminars, networking with peers, and studying the lessons of market legends are all ways to expand your knowledge and refine your approach. By staying curious and open-minded, you ensure that your skills and strategies remain relevant in a constantly changing environment.

Long-term success also requires aligning your financial achievements with your broader life goals. Money is a means to an end, not an end in itself, and true success involves using your financial resources to create a life that is rich in purpose and fulfillment. This might mean building a retirement fund that allows you to pursue your passions, creating a legacy for your family, or supporting causes that matter to you.

Financial success also brings responsibilities, such as managing wealth effectively and making decisions that reflect your values. This might involve working with financial advisors, tax professionals, or estate planners to ensure that your wealth is protected and aligned with your goals. It also involves giving back whether through philanthropy, mentorship, or other forms of contribution recognizing that true wealth is measured not just in dollars but in the positive impact you make.

Sustaining success in the market is not about perfection but persistence. It's about recognizing that setbacks are part of the journey and approaching each challenge with resilience and determination. It's about staying humble in the face of success and open to learning from others. Most importantly, it's about staying true to your values and ensuring that your achievements enhance your life and the lives of those around you.

As you reflect on your journey, remember that the market is a long game. Success is not defined by a single trade or even a single year but by the cumulative impact of your decisions over decades. By maintaining discipline, staying adaptable, and focusing on your long-term goals, you position yourself not only to succeed but to thrive in the ever-changing world of finance.

The principles and practices outlined in this book are just the beginning. The true journey begins with action putting what you've learned into practice, refining your approach, and committing yourself to the process of growth. The market is a challenging and rewarding arena, and with the right mindset and tools, you can navigate its complexities with confidence and purpose.

Sustaining success in the financial markets is not just a technical endeavor; it is a holistic pursuit that requires mental, emotional, and even philosophical balance. Beyond charts, strategies, and analysis, your ability to maintain long-term success depends on how well you manage your mindset, adapt to change, and integrate your market activities into a fulfilling life. This chapter delves deeper into these dimensions, offering practical guidance and timeless principles for thriving over the long haul.

One of the most important aspects of playing the long game is cultivating resilience. Markets are inherently volatile, and even the most carefully crafted strategies will face periods of underperformance. Resilience allows you to stay the course during these challenging times, maintaining confidence in your approach while being open to adjustments. This resilience stems from preparation: having a diversified portfolio, a well-defined plan, and a clear understanding of your risk tolerance. It also comes from recognizing that setbacks are not failures but opportunities to learn and grow.

A long-term perspective also involves embracing the concept of delayed gratification. In a world where instant results are often celebrated, the ability to delay gratification is a rare and powerful trait. Investors like Warren Buffett and Anne Scheiber exemplify this principle, achieving extraordinary wealth through decades of compounding and disciplined reinvestment. The key is to focus on the process rather than the outcome, trusting that consistent effort and smart decisions will yield rewards over time.

To support this long-term focus, it is essential to manage expectations. Markets do not move in straight lines, and periods of strong performance are often followed by corrections or stagnation. Unrealistic expectations can lead to frustration, impulsive decisions, and even burnout. By setting realistic goals and measuring progress over years rather than months, you can maintain a healthier relationship with the market. Celebrate incremental progress and view periods of underperformance as part of the natural rhythm of investing.

Another critical factor in sustaining success is financial discipline. This extends beyond the market to your broader financial habits. Maintaining a budget, managing debt, and building an emergency fund create a stable foundation that allows you to invest with confidence. Financial discipline also involves understanding the role of taxes, fees, and expenses in shaping your returns. By minimizing costs and maximizing tax efficiency, you preserve more of your hard-earned gains and allow your portfolio to grow more effectively.

Adaptability is another cornerstone of long-term success. The financial markets are dynamic, shaped by technological advancements, regulatory changes, and evolving economic conditions. Strategies that worked in the past may no longer be effective, requiring you to remain flexible and open to new ideas. For instance, the rise of algorithmic trading, the growth of cryptocurrencies, and the increasing popularity of environmental, social, and governance (ESG) investing have all created new opportunities and challenges for market participants. Staying informed about these trends and being willing to adjust your approach ensures that you remain competitive and relevant.

Technology plays a significant role in sustaining market success. From portfolio management software to algorithmic trading tools, technology can enhance your efficiency, reduce errors, and provide valuable insights. However, it is important to use technology as a complement to your skills and judgment, not a substitute.

The best investors leverage technology to support their strategies while retaining control over key decisions.

Equally important is the role of **emotional intelligence** in navigating the markets. Emotional intelligence involves recognizing and managing your emotions, understanding the emotions of others, and using this awareness to guide your actions. Fear and greed are the two dominant emotions in the market, and the ability to control them is critical to making rational decisions. For example, resisting the urge to sell during a market downturn requires emotional discipline, as does avoiding the temptation to chase speculative bubbles. By cultivating emotional intelligence, you become better equipped to stay calm under pressure and make decisions that align with your long-term goals.

To sustain success, it is also vital to **align your financial activities with your personal values and aspirations**. Money is a tool that should enhance your life, not dominate it. Reflect on why you are pursuing financial success and how it fits into the bigger picture. Are you building wealth to retire early, support your family, fund philanthropic endeavors, or pursue creative passions? By clarifying your "why," you create a sense of purpose that motivates you to stay disciplined and focused.

Philanthropy is one way to align your market achievements with a greater purpose. Many successful investors, from Warren Buffett to Ray Dalio, have committed significant portions of their wealth to charitable causes. Giving back not only benefits society but also provides personal fulfillment and a sense of legacy. Whether it's through donations, impact investing, or mentoring the next generation of traders, contributing to the greater good enriches your financial journey.

As you reflect on your journey, remember that sustaining success is not about perfection but about persistence. It's about showing up consistently, learning from every experience, and staying true to your principles. It's also about maintaining balance ensuring that your financial pursuits enhance your life rather than consuming it. Taking time to nurture relationships, pursue hobbies, and enjoy the fruits of your labor is as important as achieving financial milestones.

Finally, sustaining success requires a commitment to **lifelong learning**. The markets are a constant source of challenges and opportunities, and staying curious and engaged ensures that you continue to grow. Read widely, seek out diverse perspectives, and never stop questioning your assumptions. The more you learn, the more prepared you will be to adapt to change and seize opportunities.

The long game is not a sprint but a marathon, and success is measured not just by financial gains but by the quality of the life you create. By integrating the principles of resilience, discipline, adaptability, and purpose into your market journey, you position yourself to achieve sustainable success that supports your broader aspirations. The market is an incredible arena of opportunity, and with the right mindset and tools, you can navigate it with confidence, clarity, and purpose.

Reviews

1. A Must-Read for Every Nigerian Investor

"Winning the Market Game" is a game-changer! As a Nigerian, I've often felt disconnected from the complexities of global markets, but this book made everything clear and relatable. The emphasis on discipline and mindset really hit home for me. It's not just about making money; it's about creating opportunities for financial freedom. It is highly recommended for anyone ready to take control of their finances!
— Emeka Nnedu

2. Practical, Insightful, and Empowering

This book is a breath of fresh air for Nigerians looking to understand the financial markets. The author does an incredible job of breaking down complex concepts into practical steps anyone can follow. Whether you're a beginner or have some experience, "Winning the Market Game" provides strategies that work in any market environment, including ours here in Nigeria. A fantastic resource!
— Fatima Kabir

3. Finally, a Guide That Speaks to Us

I've read several books on investing, but none felt as relatable as this one. The author's insights resonate with the unique challenges we face in Nigeria, like economic volatility and limited access to resources. "Winning the Market Game" shows that success is not about luck or privilege but about strategy and persistence. It's a must-read for every Nigerian looking to win at the market game!
— Tunde Osunde

4. Perfect for Nigerian Entrepreneurs and Investors

As a business owner in Nigeria, I always felt investing in the markets was too risky. This book changed my perspective entirely. The chapters on risk management and developing a personalized strategy were especially valuable. I now feel confident enough to take the first steps toward building a portfolio. This book is empowering, insightful, and a true guide for Nigerians aspiring to grow their wealth.
— Chinelo Eze

5. A Guide to Financial Freedom for Nigerians

"Winning the Market Game" is not just a book; it's a blueprint for achieving financial independence. The author's emphasis on mindset, strategy, and adaptability is exactly what we need in Nigeria, where market conditions can be unpredictable. I've already started applying the lessons, and I can see the difference in how I approach investments. This book is worth every naira!
— Ahmed Sanu

About The Book

Unlock the Secrets to Financial Success

The stock market can seem like a daunting maze, reserved for the lucky or the elite. But with the right mindset, strategy, and tools, anyone can succeed. *Winning the Market Game* is your guide to understanding the markets, developing a personalized approach, and navigating risks with confidence.

Discover how to master market psychology, build effective strategies, and learn from legendary investors. Whether you're starting out or refining your skills, this book offers actionable insights to help you thrive in any market condition.

Ready to take control of your financial future? Open the book and start winning today.

About The Author

Adedeji Sunmola is a passionate financial educator, seasoned trader, and advocate for financial literacy. With years of experience navigating the complexities of global and local markets, Adedeji has dedicated his career to helping individuals take control of their financial futures. His practical approach, rooted in discipline, strategy, and adaptability, has empowered countless people to demystify the markets and make informed investment decisions.

Born and raised in Nigeria, Adedeji understands the unique challenges and opportunities faced by investors in emerging markets. He combines a deep knowledge of global financial systems with an intimate understanding of the local economic landscape, providing insights that resonate with readers from all walks of life. Through his writing, workshops, and mentorship programs, he has inspired individuals to build wealth, achieve financial freedom, and embrace the market as a tool for personal and economic empowerment.

Winning the Market Game is Adedeji's debut book, a culmination of years of experience, reflection, and a desire to make the world of investing accessible to everyone. When he's not writing or trading, Adedeji enjoys mentoring young entrepreneurs, exploring innovative investment strategies, and spending time with his family. He believes that financial success is not just about money but about creating a life of purpose, freedom, and impact.

www.ingramcontent.com/pod-product-compliance
Lightning Source LLC
LaVergne TN
LVHW091530070526
838199LV00001B/9